BOOKS BY HUGH SIDEY

*A Very Personal Presidency: Lyndon Johnson
in the White House*   *1968*

John F. Kennedy, President   *1963, 1964*

A VERY
PERSONAL
PRESIDENCY

HUGH SIDEY

A VERY PERSONAL PRESIDENCY

*Lyndon Johnson
in the White House*

ATHENEUM
NEW YORK
1968

To Cindy, Sandy and Tina Sidey

AUTHOR'S NOTE

THIS IS A BOOK of glimpses. None is a total by itself, but it is my hope that when put together in the reader's mind, much like the frames of a motion picture, they will leave a full and fresh impression, perhaps even bring new understanding, of Lyndon Johnson's Presidency.

This is not a biography of that extraordinary man. It is not a definitive history nor is it a complete narrative of his stewardship. It is a sketch of his tumultuous years in the White House. This book is the distillation of almost two million words of research which I have written about the man over the years in which, as a Washington correspondent, I have studied him as intensely as I have studied any man on the national scene. This is not an authorized volume. No special favors were asked of the White House or of Johnson. None were granted.

In these pages are what I saw and heard and the opinions I formed from the exhaustive reporting which began back in 1957 when I started to write about the United States Senate and I hesitantly walked into the office of the Majority Leader. I was at Dallas for the tragic beginning of this 36th Presidency. I have followed it since then from the dusty streets of Johnson City, Texas, to the cool quiet of the Oval Office in the White

House and on around the world to a dozen places of the highest political drama.

Few of the major events of Johnson's Presidency have run their course. It is too early for profound assessment, and it would be foolhardy to look far into the future. I have tried here, instead, to relate Johnson in a new way to the major phenomena of his Presidency, explaining not so much the sequence of events as why he arrived at the decisions he made, what he thought and said and sought, and the aura he produced.

I discovered several basic patterns in his Presidency while sorting through so much raw material, and this helped shape the book. Johnson governs in spasms—he conducts great orgies of activity, either in response to a challenge or in support of his proposals. These are followed by weeks and months of quiet—times of brooding and evaluation. And the record shows that once he has set a course, he is reluctant to change it. He is repetitive in his thinking, in his technique of governing, and even in his language. There is a certain rote, too, in his approaches to problems that may appear to be similar. Thus, I felt it was possible to select certain peaks and valleys in the Johnson graph of the past four years and, in writing about them, offer some new insight into the entire profile of his Presidency.

It has been an utterly fascinating journey. It also has been a humbling one. The dimensions of the Presidential burden awe anyone who watches closely. Any comment on the man who has the courage to seek and the skill to serve in the Presidency is in a way presumptuous.

And yet the office needs and demands constant examination and discussion. That is essential to our national health. The challenge is to be diligent in the pursuit of the facts and then to be calm in their consideration and, finally, to be fair in their application. I have tried to do all those things in this book.

ACKNOWLEDGMENTS

THERE ARE THOUSANDS to whom I bow for help along this intense journey. First I must thank President and Mrs. Johnson and the hundreds in their official family who have been so tolerant of me over these years. To those in other parts of the government and on many sides of the issues, I also want to express my appreciation for befriending me in my efforts to know what happened. My superiors Dick Clurman and John Steele were understanding and encouraging. My colleagues were helpful and patient. I have a special indebtedness to Penny Marshall, who chased elusive facts, and editor Mike Bessie, who waited so cheerfully. Finally, a tribute to my wife, Anne, who endured—no light task.

CONTENTS

A VERY
PERSONAL
PRESIDENCY

LEGEND

Lyndon Johnson's restored Boyhood Home is the best reflection of the man that has yet been created. Its façade is feigned to a noticeable degree, representing not so much the home in which the President used to live as the home that he wishes he had lived in. The little house sparkles now, a recipient of all the marvelous ministrations that big-city television money can muster. From a block down Avenue G when you first turn off U.S. Highway 290, a boring slash of concrete that wandered into nowhere until a President was discovered living by it, the Boyhood Home shines in its new white paint, a beacon in the dusty environs of Johnson City, population 611 by the last census but now probably close to 850 by the estimate of Mayor George E. Byars, a kindly, wrinkled man of agile mind who preaches the glories of his town with the ardor of a Miami Jaycee.

The walls of the little plains home run plumb now, showing none of the weather-weariness that crept into the rafters almost from the day it was finished in 1886.

The big-city carpenters did a good job of hammering out the sags, which is sad in a way since they were a testimonial to suffering and at this distance in time suffering can be noble. Before Lady Bird marched in with her cheerful restorative legions, the grasshoppers had eaten the paint, the great summer heat which sears and clutches and chokes had laid its hand on the roof, and the blizzards had roared unobstructed out of the north to pound and slice at the frail flanks. Weather was almost as bad as economics during the boyhood days of Lyndon Johnson, and those two massive forces worked incessantly on the people and on the buildings.

The white paint and the new siding cover the scars. The roof is new, the gray shutters are trim and straight, and on the back, where new walls were raised to encase the family artifacts laid out inside, the windows are aluminized. Below them a huge General Electric air-conditioner pours its soothing breeze inside.

When the President visits his ranch just fifteen miles on down the road, he comes by to look the home over. He ambles up over great slabs of thick, new concrete, and inevitably he pauses by the old well in the front yard, which has been crisply caulked into picture-book quaintness. Johnson scans the live oaks, which had endured, broken and splintered, for decades but stand now with new respectability if not authenticity. Their wounds have been treated, their broken branches removed. A sturdy split-rail fence encloses the whole block, and it is entwined with delicate creeping red roses. The lawn, too, has received the benefits of all the horticultural innovations, and it sprouts lush and green when the spring rains come, or even if they don't, which is often the case in Texas.

In the back yard are the water tank and the old windmill, which cling to memories even if the loud-speaker system that hangs from the tree branches, the modernistic streetlights and the wheeled dolly for the garbage cans do not. Everything is a reminder of the man who ordered it preserved even before he became President. Where the old has endured—in the front porch with its gingerbread trim and potted ferns, in the limestone foundation and chimneys—there is harmony from a single age. But where technology offered conven-ience, as in the spotlights under the eaves, the style is Pedernales Renaissance.

The sight is not unpleasing, nor is it even preten-tious. It is just not the way it used to be when Lyndon Johnson grew to manhood. The creation is designed for popular consumption. It is another prop on that clut-tered stage which the 36th President of the United States has created. But as with all of Johnson's creations—and he is his own best work—to stop at the trim gate and only look is to fail to understand. The meaning is within, and it does not come easily.

The interior of that house, like the exterior, is glam-orized and polished and encased and framed so that there is a pleasant sense of care and middle-class means. It is in proper taste, and with its Victorian sofa with the red velvet seat and the needlepoint cushions on the chairs there is the feel of the 1920's. But the first glance

5

offers nothing really unusual for the visitor. One must pause and linger and read the old letters and study the brown photographs on the walls. Only then does one begin to feel the pinch of those tiny rooms, and only then does Lyndon Johnson begin to emerge in one's mind.

This house was the home of Lyndon Johnson for most of his school years, and in many ways it still is home. He returns and returns, hands in his pockets, loitering like a boy, remembering with amazing accuracy the sights and sounds. He cannot stay away long. Not even his ranch can bring him the same sustenance. The ranch was something he built after he had become a multimillionaire and one of the nation's most powerful political men. But the Boyhood Home built him.

It was the home of Sam Ealy Johnson, Jr., and Rebekah Baines Johnson, but even the most casual observer can tell in a few minutes of quiet contemplation of the inside exhibits that Sam Ealy was not the one who counted the most. A Texas hat, it is true, hangs on the hatrack and Sam Ealy appears in the sequence of family album photographs. But as one progresses through the small chambers, he fades away and Rebekah's presence fills the space and the mind. A Southern matriarch, college-educated and surprisingly cultivated for the scorched and poverty-worn environs of Johnson City, she was utterly determined not only to squeeze from her meager surroundings what happiness there was but to mold her oldest son into something neither her husband nor her father had ever been.

6

The bookstand with Shakespeare and Whittier and the writings of Thomas Jefferson, forming a fine but tenuous thread to a glorious world far beyond, speaks of Rebekah and so does the wind-up phonograph.

There was poetry in that amazing woman. She wrote about the day of her eldest son's birth, "Now the light came in from the east, bringing a deep stillness, a stillness so profound and so pervasive that it seemed as if the earth itself were listening." She was unabashed by such outpouring. Novelist Sherry Kafka, the daughter of one of the pastors of the First Baptist Church, Rebekah's house of worship, walked the dusty streets of Johnson City gathering material for her book *Hannah Jackson,* and as she writes of her fictionalized Hannah, she also describes Rebekah. "Few of us," says one of the figures in the novel, "ever have the courage to live as though they understand the ways of men. And only a tiny elect dare live as though they understand the ways of God. That was how Hannah Jackson lived." Rebekah could lift herself out of the dreariness of her life and stand on a magnificent stage where she and her family walked and talked and lived among the great men and women of the age. Her oldest son, Lyndon, can still recall the moments when fatigue and discouragement would overwhelm Rebekah, but they never defeated her. The vision persisted until that day in 1958 when she died. By then her firstborn had become Majority Leader of the United States Senate, which was gratifying but not really beyond her farthest calculations.

It perhaps would be unfair to suggest there was un-

7

happiness in the Boyhood Home of Lyndon Johnson. But at least there was at times the feeling of hopelessness and a deep-down unrest that manifested itself in the letters which the boy and mother exchanged. Always there was the gentle urging, between the lines if no place else, to go beyond Johnson City and Texas, to strike out, to somehow escape the world of constant worry and concern which Rebekah and Sam had known. There is one curious paradox in this, however. By Johnson City standards, the Johnsons were far from destitute. Indeed, they ranked in the aristocracy of that town by blood and even by income and position when Sam was a state legislator. Yet in comparison to the world beyond, which Rebekah had sensed from family and scholarship, they had very little. Johnson City had very little. This was Texas before the impact of the oil fortunes, and it was, in worldly terms, almost nothing. The phenomenon is important. Lyndon Johnson's mind was conditioned to leadership, to the thought that he belonged on top by dint of ancestry and, as school proved to him, by his mind. Had he gone to school where competition was more severe, he might not have been so convinced of his natural superiority, which was real enough. But there was nothing to slow him down, really, within his limited sphere. He swept all before him from early infancy—at least, that is the way his mother chronicled it, and she is just about the only authority on those days. He learned the alphabet from blocks before he was two, could spell and do some reading by the time he was four. His grades were superior from the start, and he graduated from high school at the head of his class and the elected president of those few. He was bigger than just about anybody else not only in stature but in achievement. Had there been more than six persons in his senior class, he might not have found his dominance so effortless, since he rarely studied but found time for a goodly number of pranks as well as after-school work. There were no organized athletics in his small school, and so a natural lack of physical skill never embarrassed him or detracted from his triumphs as a debater. He had the chance in his small high school and college to try his hand at virtually everything— journalism, student politics, drama and debate. This is a phenomenon of the small community. A person with ability not only has the chance to test himself in a broad spectrum of society's activities, but often feels obligated because there are so few others to serve. Virtuosity does not often develop in such a clime, but interests do. A student has time to sample and choose. It was very plain not only to others but to Lyndon Johnson himself that he was of superior clay, quick to grasp meaning, excelling at whatever he tried, relishing authority. There was no need to believe that the rest of the world would be different. This state of mind was the legacy of Johnson City and of the tiny home run by Rebekah Baines Johnson. That is why the Boyhood Home tells so much.

Some small-town wonders falter when they get into the big arena. A surprising number do not. Having resided in their own aristocracy, they are loath to take second place elsewhere. Their answer is to work harder and then harder. The high ranks of industry are peopled with men of such background. Lyndon Johnson is an even more towering example.

Yet, while understanding his own right to leadership, he also sensed very early that the world had not been fair to him in material matters. There was no fat bank account, nor was there any opulence. Those old pictures on the walls show the family assembled in the traditional rituals of rural America. They gathered around one of the early automobiles to add novelty to the snapshots and some sense of worldliness to their family history. Even the photographs seem hot and dusty, the children standing barefoot in the dirt, the adults rumpled but determinedly leading a picnic, which was the entertainment staple of that age. There was not much else.

Lady Bird's diligent researchers uncovered a series of photos of the early Johnson City, and the scene is even more stark. Rutted dirt streets are lined with rickety buildings, and tilted telephone poles offer the only shade. When viewed inside the Boyhood Home air-cooled by General Electric, there seems to be a sense of adventure about that life. Only those who lived it know the truth. Lyndon Johnson had gone to Austin many times and played around the desk of his father, who was a state legislator for twelve years. The great Sam Rayburn, who had been Speaker of the House in the Texas Legislature, went on to Congress, and it may be that Johnson's restlessness began that early. The view of larger things was tantalizing. There was, however, still a great distance to go.

One of the letters carefully encased on the back porch was written by Johnson when he was a student at Southwest Texas State Teachers College in San Marcos. "Dear Grandmother," he wrote in February of 1927, "When I was home several weeks ago mother gave me a box with some clothes in it that you had sent for me. . . . You don't know how I appreciate the interest that you have always manifested in our little family and I am looking forward to the day when I can reciprocate. The suits both fit me and I wear them every day. I haven't had any new clothes since I started to school and these sure are handy. . . ."

If there was no resentment, then he must at least have wondered why he had not been dealt with more generously. This wonderment was a common Texas syndrome that grew to astounding proportions as isolation, both national and regional, faded before the New Deal and then the onslaught of Hitler. In its simplest form, it became a chip on the shoulder, a resentment against just about anybody beyond the Texas borders—all non-Texans were considered to be more blessed than Texans and suspected of harboring secret loathings of anything Texan. There may have been some justification for that feeling among Texans, but not to the extent that it was nurtured by many, including Lyndon Johnson.

In the Boyhood Home there is another letter which signals what was to come in Johnson. It is a letter to his mother showing the strength of their attachment and his feeling that life has not been fair to her. And there is that incipient chip on the shoulder, the I'm-going-to-make-it-right determination. Mother and son must have been in perfect phase.

"My Dear Mother," he wrote, "The end of another busy day brought me a letter from you. Your letters always give me more strength renewed courage and that bulldog tenacity so essential to the success of any man. There is no force that exerts the power over me that your letters do. I have learned to look forward to them so long and now when one is delayed a spell of sadness and disappointment is cast over me.

"I have been thinking of you all afternoon. As I passed through town on my way home to supper I could see the mothers doing their Xmas shopping. It made me wish for my mother so much. I thought of the hard times that you always have in seeing that every child is supplied with a gift from mother. I hope the years to come will place me in a position where I can relieve you of the hardships that it has fallen your lot to suffer— and I'm going to begin on a small scale right now. The enclosed is very small but you can make it go a long way. I don't guess daddy has found me a job—so I may not get home for the holidays. I'll be thinking of all of you every minute. I love you so much, Your son . . ."

Finally, there is one other document that deserves attention. It, too, is a letter, the one written by Rebekah to her son when he was first elected to Congress. The election was the release, that joyous entry into the world of her dreams, the way out that neither her father nor she had found. "To me your election not alone gratifies my pride as a mother in a splendid and satisfying son and delights me with the realization of the joy you must feel in your success but in a measure it compensates for the heartache and disappointment I experienced as a child when my dear father lost the race you have just won. The confidence in the good judgment of the people was sadly shattered then by their choice of another man. Today my faith is restored. How happy it would have made my precious noble father to know that the firstborn of his firstborn would achieve the position he desired. It makes me happy to have you carry on the ideals and principles so cherished by that great and good man. I gave you his name. I commend you to his example. You have always justified my expectations, my hopes, my dreams. How dear to me you are you cannot know my darling boy, my devoted son, my strength and comfort. . . . Always remember that I love you and am behind you in all that comes to you. . . ."

In the first three years that the Boyhood Home was open to the public, some 200,000 tourists came with their Brownie cameras, snapped the kids' pictures on the front fence and then took the five-minute tour which is conducted by the ladies of Johnson City and their teen-age daughters. For the most part, they stood silent and rather bored, since what they saw was so very commonplace. It was not rustic enough to conjure up images of Indians and cowboys, and it was so far from the baronial mansions of the East, or even of Texas, that the tourists could not be awed. Nevertheless, more of Lyndon Johnson is evident in that home than in any other surviving family monument.

Standing in the side yard amid the pecan trees and the live oaks, one can look over the low roofs of Johnson City toward the endless horizon. Only the cupola of the Blanco County Court House, a solid mound of native limestone, and George Croft's sheet-metal feed elevator dare challenge that horizon. The country then rolls off endlessly.

It is easy to oversimplify Johnson. He has lived longer in Washington, D.C., than anyplace else. He knows, by actual count, more Congressmen and Senators than he does residents of Johnson City. But all that still does not erase—indeed, it has strengthened—the bond to his hometown. In almost every action that Johnson takes today as President there is a strand which can be clearly followed back to his home in Texas. As a branding iron sears flesh, the memories of adolescence and early manhood in the Texas Hill Country etched themselves on Lyndon Johnson's cortex.

The lessons were all learned there. The miseries to be escaped, the mistakes to be avoided. Sometimes even today Johnson's idiom is that of the public-school playground. His humor is sprinkled with the obscenities that were the delight of juveniles in the school boys' room.

When Johnson fights poverty, his mind inevitably wanders back to his first shock at seeing the Mexican-American children of Texas rummaging through the garbage cans of a roadhouse looking for grapefruit rinds.

He can tell in improved detail, as time passes, how Johnson City was integrated. It is a basic story in the Johnson repertoire. A young road foreman named Melvin Winters came to town with a gang of Negro construction workers. They camped along the Pedernales River, and that night Winters came to the barber shop for a hair cut. He was confronted by the town bully, who, according to LBJ, told Winters to get "his niggers" out of town before sundown. Winters refused. And as he was stepping down from the barber's chair he caught the heel of his Texas boot on the footrest and fell forward. At the same time the bully swung hard from the floor, catching Winters on the chin and knocking him out. "They threw a bucket of water in his face," says Johnson when he warms to his topic, "and when he came to, Melvin went out in the street and fought. They fought for an hour and a half. The street was roped off and the people gathered and finally Melvin had the bully down on the street and was banging his head against the concrete curb [Johnson grasps an imaginary victim and smashes his head on the paving] and he was saying, 'Do my niggers stay, do my niggers stay?' and finally the bully says, 'Yes.' That's the way that Johnson City was integrated and it's been that way ever since." Melvin, now a successful Johnson City highway contractor, smiles when asked about the story. He does not deny it, but he hardly looks like the John Wayne whom Johnson conjures up in his narrative. That does not matter, however. He is part of the legend and glad to serve.

Lyndon Johnson can still taste the dust when he wants to, and he can still feel that merciless sun and scan the horizon and worry because water won't come. His acute sensitivity to water comes from those young days. He recalls the time when his father was in the State Legislature and the Hill Country was scorched into a deep brown by a giant sun that was never challenged by clouds. Just about everything dried and shriveled and blew away—everything except the men, and they somehow stayed on the land. But morning after morning they would come to Johnson City before the sun rose to do its hideous work, and some of them, unshaven and hollow-eyed, would come carrying their broad-brimmed hats up to Sam Johnson's home, and young Lyndon Johnson would be awakened by the scrape of their boots across the wooden porch outside his bedroom window and he could hear their voices, thinned by the heat, asking if Sam Johnson could somehow help them get water for what livestock they had left living. He is quite convinced that adequate water in the areas of shortage and control of the water in the areas of surplus could do more for peace than just about any technological breakthrough. The world is simply Johnson City in megatons.

When he talks of it, his voice grows quiet and he is far away. "I guess that from my earliest memory, because I was born and raised just a stone's throw from a river, I have felt that our future was limited only by our water supply. . . . Water was the determining factor in our happiness down there. When the rains came and

when the water collected, the waterholes filled up and
the rivers were full, and there was happiness. We could
use the water on the land to make crops grow and the
animals could drink. When there was drouth or floods
came, things were horrible. . . . My neighbor had five
feet of water in his house and his car was washed away
as late as 1952. Lady Bird was up all night long once
when the water was creeping up in the front yard of the
ranch, and I've been up all night several times moving
tractors and equipment to get it out of the way of floods.
. . . The first part of my legislative life was spent on
building six dams along the Colorado, taming it, har-
nessing it. . . . I have to laugh at how some of these
immature kids now say that I want everybody to love
me. I never had everybody love me. They hated me for
these dams. The power companies gave me hell. They
called me a communist. . . . And now they have water
and power down there and no floods and the land went
up from $6 an acre to $160. The lakes have filled up
with homes around them, REA power lines stretch
across the land, the area has been remade. . . . They
used to have to bring water in with wagons. . . . We got
our drinking water out of cisterns. At Johnson City we
used to have to pull it out by a rope. In the summertime
the Pedernales used to run dry as a bone, not a trickle.
. . . The first thing I did when I bought my land was to
put in a dam. . . . I never had running water in a house
until I was married. . . . The prettiest sight you can
have is seeing the dam filled up on the Pedernales. And
one of the nicest sounds you can have is hearing the

water at night going over that dam."

If there was anything else which impressed itself with such force on Johnson's mind and carried over from that small home, it was the need for strong women. All those characteristics which he had sensed in his mother he looked for and found in his wife. "I outmarried myself," he insists today. "She's my strength." Indeed, Lady Bird is even more than Rebekah. She is almost unreal. Controlled, determined, subdued, kindly, intelligent, dedicated. As in Rebekah, there is sensitivity in Lady Bird, even poetry, and it comes out when she talks of that land. "The sun is indomitable. You know if it is cloudy now the sun will come out in the next day or two. I fell in love with the Texas Hill Country before I met Lyndon. It was good courting country—a lot of wonderful places for picnics. I like the long twilight. I like the long horizon. You are part of the sky. There are lovely sunsets and at night you seem closer . . . the stars are so clear and bright."

The daughters, Lynda Bird and Luci Baines, now married young women, are the next step in this enduring strain. They have been taught to stand by themselves. They were called upon as teen-agers to give short political speeches. They were companions for a worried President later. Luci took her father to pray one night in his brooding about sending bombers to strike the oil-storage areas of North Vietnam. Johnson was deeply gratified that Lynda rushed from the University of Texas to comfort the children of Governor John Connally, who was severely wounded that day in Dallas.

18

"I'm the luckiest man alive," the President says. "None of my girls drinks or smokes or takes dope and they both married fine men."

Always he could recall the suffering. Those who had to pump water and chop wood and light their way with kerosene lamps "aged before their time." He remembers line by line the dialogue between himself and his father when the elder Johnson, suffering from heart disease, got out of his bed in an Austin hospital and demanded to be taken back among his people to die. There were no modern medical facilities in the tiny town, but Sam Ealy wanted to be where "they care if you are sick and they know if you die." Johnson has vowed he will do what he can so others do not have to go through such ordeals.

The economic lesson of those early years, as related later when Johnson was in the White House, was that the bankers controlled the land and the people and the dreams. The banker was king. The image was one of "the man who lived in the big white house up on the hill." Curiously, Johnson did not seem to resent the possession of economic power. He just wanted to be the one to have it. When big wealth became his, LBJ bought up banks and land, and he still is doing it today. It is a kind of insurance against those terrible Populist memories of high interest and mortgage foreclosures and the stock-market break. Land only is enduring.

If there was one thing better than money in Johnson City, it was education, and only because it was the key to money and to power and the outside world. Rebekah

Baines Johnson was different and better because she was a college graduate, and if the interminable sermon she preached her eldest son about going to school did not register fully at the time, it did later. Glimpsed from beyond, the one thing which unlocked all that human energy of Johnson's was the realization one cold evening after working on the road gang all day for one dollar that his mother was right about a college degree. He went off to San Marcos and Southwest Texas State Teachers College and, to hear him tell it, the rest was inevitable.

If long ago the frontier had faded in Blanco County, Texas, the legend had not and fierceness was a part of every boy's heritage. Hunting and fishing were fundamental skills that came before baseball and football. Toughness was to be shown, if in no other way, then through the mouth. Some observers now call this affliction the "Alamo syndrome" and it has to do with the idea that a man must fight in one way or another to get what he wants. It is a legend of turmoil and trouble in a way, but its mark is unmistakably there. Courage is to stand tall and stare a man down; to dominate and direct and mold everything and everybody; to preach and expect obedience. Johnson had a lot of legend to listen to and live up to. He remembered it all. His great-uncle and his grandfather drove cattle up to Abilene, Kansas. And he believes that they were the hardiest characters around. At least they endured and they left a town in their name. LBJ invokes frequently in his monologues what he claims are pioneer axioms.

"He's a good man to go to the well with," says Johnson, explaining that in the Indian era two persons had to go to the communal water supply—one to draw the water and the other to watch out for marauding Indians, who used to wait at the waterholes for their enemies. The other version is "He's a good man to get behind a log with," and that carries precisely the same connotation—when you are lying behind a log, presumably battling Indians, you want the stoutest of hearts beside you.

The President relishes the story of his grandmother and her experience with the Indians. There are, naturally, several versions. The most complete one, which can be a good ten-minute story when Johnson is in the best of form, has it that his grandmother Eliza Bunton Johnson was left alone one day by her husband, who had gone off with others in the settlement to chase some errant Comanches. With one child and one infant she had gone to the spring for water when she saw an Indian raiding party come over the horizon. She rushed back to the cabin, took both children into a fruit cellar and covered the outlines of the door with a rug. To prevent the child from crying, she tied a diaper over its mouth, and the baby she put to her breast to nurse. The Indians entered and tore up the cabin interior some, but did not detect the pioneer woman, who remained in hiding for hours until she heard her husband return and call out anxiously for her. Then, only hesitating for a minute in her own relief, she went on to care for the men wounded in their fight with the Indians. Fight and endure is the lesson, and fight some more.

Texas' great historian Walter Prescott Webb, a friend of Johnson's, fueled the fires of legend with marvelous stories that had the added virtue of being wholly true. It was not lost on the Johnson City populace that Webb wrote that "the battle of the Pedernales has good claims to being the first battle in which the six-shooter was used on mounted Indians." The date is fixed roughly in the spring of 1844 and, of course, the Texas Rangers are the heroes, riding out of San Antonio into the Hill Country to shoot down more than thirty Indians with Samuel Colt's revolutionary new weapon. Until then Indians used to strike after their enemies had discharged their guns and were defenseless as they went through the clumsy reloading procedure. But along the Pedernales on that fateful day the Comanches were stunned when the Rangers first fired their rifles and then leaped on their horses and attacked, firing their revolvers from the saddle. Life changed and legend grew.

"Know the difference between a Texas Ranger and a Sheriff?" Lyndon Johnson once asked some journalists who walked with him through the Boyhood Home just before it was opened to the public. "When you shoot a Ranger, he just keeps comin' on," said the President, leafing through a book on the Rangers.

The wellspring of courage was the Alamo. Less than a hundred miles from Johnson City. The ultimate in human courage and sacrifice. The glittering names— Davy Crockett, Jim Bowie, William Travis, James Bonham. Lyndon Johnson longed for some blood connection to those dead heroes, but he had none. Finally, that did not stop him, and when he was talking to the troops in Korea in 1966 he boldly claimed that he had had a great-great-grandfather who died at the Alamo. It was something that should have been, at least in Johnson's mind, and so he just said it was so. That he might not be counted among the courageous was a persistent worry of LBJ's. Perhaps it is of all men who reach the top. John Kennedy was obsessed with the chemistry of courage. Johnson's was that Texas brand which still had bullets and knives and bad guys. When Johnson won a Silver Star for his coolness under fire in the South Pacific in World War II, he put the rosette of the decoration in his lapel and he never has been without it. "Surely," he said when he was debating whether to fly to South Vietnam to review American troops in 1966, "I don't have to demonstrate my physical courage." But he did, at least to himself, and he knew it. The visit to Cam Ranh Bay was, in a way, a test of it, and he would not have turned his plane around as it sped from Manila over the South China Sea if all the Viet Cong in the country had been reported converging on the city. How much the "Alamo syndrome" enters into Johnson's conduct of foreign policy is debatable, but it is there. It is perhaps measurable in the President's response to the Dominican Republic uprising. Ten thousand troops might have been United States presence enough, but before Johnson called a halt there were twenty-four thousand ashore. The sheer weight of

23

their numbers clouded what was otherwise a sensible and successful foreign-policy response.

If life is direct and open and fundamental in Johnson City, so is death. It is a part of that life. Urban America and suburbia and all the other thick clusters of residence in today's society stratify people in just about every way—by income, by age, by health, by birth. Some persons can reach adulthood having never seen or felt death at close range. There is no such isolation in a small town. Illness and age exist beside health and youth. The funerals of those who have lived long and quietly can be almost social occasions, to which the friends come to remember and dab their eyes as custom requires. The sorrow is deep, but it is bearable because all these people, when they are first old enough to reason, understand that death is there—inevitable, sometimes tragic, but sometimes almost comforting, always inevitable. Death is daily and weekly and among friends and enemies. There is a normalcy about death in this close context, and it becomes part of the commerce and the talk and the sight of life. It is felt, certainly, but it is accepted with equanimity. Lyndon Johnson could so accept death. I remember once sitting in his office when he was Majority Leader of the Senate and he had just learned of the tragic death of the daughter of John Connally, then a Texas attorney. At age sixteen she had married and a few days later been killed by the accidental discharge of her husband's gun when they were in a Florida apartment. Johnson put a call through to his protégé, political ally and best friend. The words were brief and direct, almost as if the two were adding something to the Senate's agenda, business to be sandwiched in between the legislative affairs that had to march on. Only later, after pondering this conversation and its apparent lack of emotion, did it occur to me, uneasy even as a remote witness, that these two men understood the language of life and of death in a small Texas town and that, in their way, they felt as others do.

On another day—November 22, 1963—in another place—Dallas—Lyndon Johnson was to feel death profoundly, and the fact that he was no stranger in its presence helped him hold a nation together, but it also brought many to wonder what was inside the new President of the United States.

NOTES

My story of the death of a President and the beginning
of a new Presidency is in a pocket-size spiral notebook
pushed into a far corner of a lower desk drawer. It is a
chronicle of those horrifying hours in Dallas. It is a
singularly unimpressive thing to look at—ugly brown
cover, soiled, rumpled and bent. A few times over the
years, as I rummaged through those random archives, I
have suddenly come across the almost forgotten little
booklet. And each time the sight of the black grease-
pencil marking, "Kennedy Assassination," has startled
me and for a few seconds that little notebook has held
me in its malevolent spell and I have lifted it onto my
desk, tempted to go back over those agonizing minutes
again. But not until recently have I been able to do it,
and even now it is an exhausting experience.

The very extremes of human feeling are in those few
pages. The tragedy comes in that brief history so unexpectedly, so almost matter-of-factly (as it was in reality), as to be unbelievable in the opening sentences. My
first note of the incident is "Dallas" with a circle
around it. We had arrived from Fort Worth. And we
were looking for dissent. "Lets Barry King John" is my

next notation, the text taken from a protesting sign-carrier. But below that is this: "Jackie still out first." It is protocol for a President to precede everyone out of planes and doors, but most of them, when traveling with their wives, don't do that. Kennedy, however, had until then followed protocol and bolted from his airplane in the lead. But on this trip there seemed to be a special bit of warmth between the first couple—a little extra pride in John Kennedy that on this campaign journey Jackie had come along. For two stops he had gently nudged her out of Air Force One's fuselage ahead of himself. It was, in the game of President-watching, worth noting.

My limited scrawlings tell of other dissent: "Help JFK Stamp Out Democracy." And there was one totally baffling placard which was noted because it made no sense: "2 or 4 legs: swims, walks, flies or crawls, Anything but JFK." And once again there is happiness on a sunny day. "Jackie at Fence" was my shorthand reminder of how Mrs. Kennedy went to the airport fence, which she rarely did, and shook hands like a true politician.

It was so wonderfully joyous—and normal—that the only note taken until disaster was this: "Motorcade—Main Street." That ended one of those tiny pages and the entry at the top of the next page is the beginning of horror, but it plainly was put down before I had full comprehension of that day's shattering event. "Triple underpass—west edge of town—Main, Elm, Commerce converge—bright sunny day." The scene was set for what we all knew could not be. Then it was. The following note was made in front of Parkland Hospital. "Jim Wright" identifies a spokesman I had never seen before and know nothing of today, but his words told the story that could never be changed. "Kennedy in head, Connally thru chest."

My handwriting grows more contorted and the story grows in anguish. "It is too horrible [from the fear-wrenched face of Senator Ralph Yarborough, who had been riding close behind the President's car] . . . SS immediately surrounded the V. Pres . . . I can't say, I can't say [cries of Yarborough to the question, Is Kennedy dead?] . . . Pres. car a lot of blood in it . . . Pres was motionless—Jackie leaning over—wheeled stretcher . . . I saw the man's head and I couldn't believe it—I nearly died—Oh my God, Oh my God [Malcolm Kilduff, assistant press secretary, sobbing aimlessly in the hospital hall] . . . White cadillac [hearse], bronze [casket]—Jackie's hand on it . . ." Each word, each dash and comma triggers a rush of memory that still leaves one limp. My ledger contains fragments of the testimony of the two young doctors who attended the President, Dr. Malcolm Perry and Dr. Kemp Clark. My notes recall again their faces, which reflected their own bludgeoning by events too big to comprehend. It was Dr. Clark, thirty-eight, who explained he had seen two wounds, one big and gaping in the head from behind, the other small and difficult to detect in the neck, but appearing to be from the front. I can recall very, very vaguely rising from my chair in that stark hospital classroom and asking Dr. Clark if he was aware that what he was saying suggested shots from two different directions and thus could bring a controversy of incalculable proportions. He could report, he said, only what appeared to him, admittedly under stress and in desperately hurried minutes when time for such observations could not be taken from the struggle to preserve an ebbing flicker of life. His words were dutifully written down.

Finally, along that tortuously scribbled trail is a three-word entry at the top of one page—"He has left." That, in my personal account of Lyndon Johnson's Presidency, was the beginning. Technically, he had been President for an hour, but this was the first moment that I could bring myself to write words, no matter how elemental, which ended something very special and began something unknown.

POWER

LYNDON JOHNSON once talked about the first hours of his Presidency:

"I entertained grave fears for our future. I didn't know if this was part of a communist conspiracy or plot against our system. . . . So in the first two hours I tried to anticipate what would flow. . . . I sat in the plane and pictured it more or less as simple as if something happened to the pilot who was flying us back. We were very much in the same shape as if he fell at the controls and one of our boys had to walk up there and bring in the plane, flying at seven hundred miles per hour with no plans showing how long the runways were, with no maps, no notes. We tried to bring it in and land there, and we went about it until about three a.m. and everybody, more or less, swung in behind me and helped to bring that plane in. . . . I wasn't sure how successful I would be in pulling the divergent factions in the country together and trying to unify and unite them in order to get the confidence of the people and secure the respect of the world. That's why I met with the Cabinet, or those of them there, and the leaders that night. That's why I talked with my individual counselors beginning at eight in the morning, and eighty-three heads of government, to the leaders of Congress, by television to the country. . . . I tried to appeal to the best in everybody, but not with my hat in hand. . . . I tried to anticipate everything that could happen. I tried to pull labor and business, the ex-Presidents, Congress, even the spiritual leaders together. People don't know it, but Billy Graham spent two or three nights in the White House. He got up at three in the morning and got down on his knees and prayed for me. At six he'd have coffee with me and we'd talk over the problems facing the country."

That is as complete an account of his thoughts in those hours as Johnson has ever given. He brushed it all aside in that perfunctory written statement he gave to the Warren Commission, covering in a few words eons of emotion. He must have almost total recall of those hours, because he does of other events far less important. It is as if he does not want to recall how it all began—that he was an accidental President.

I suspect that the three gunshots which killed John Kennedy in Dallas, the realization that Kennedy might be dead and the thought that he might be President of the United States registered with Lyndon Johnson almost instantaneously as he sat in the second car behind the death limousine. Certainly not more than a few seconds could have elapsed before the awful logic formed in his terribly keen senses and made him utterly powerless to stop thoughts that were almost obscene for the moment and certainly too big to be fully comprehended. No man of his experience, his instincts, his cunning could have, from the rear of his convertible, viewed that scene and sensed the panic and not in some way felt that the world had changed. Johnson was a hunter, used to the sound of rifle fire. The instantaneous reaction of the Secret Service agents, the sudden thrusting back of his own agent, Rufus Youngblood, to hold Johnson below door level in some manner that is not certain now in the hazy aftermath—all of this must have triggered the sense of dire emergency. Fact one—the shots—and two—the emergency—simply had to add up to the possibility that he, Lyndon Johnson, was President of the United States.

I know they did in my mind, and I was far back in the motorcade, almost drowsing with the boredom of the day and the event. The three explosions were different, just enough out of harmony with the usual clatter of motorcycle exhaust backfires to touch something way down deep and release in that fragmented second a series of truncated thoughts that tumbled over each other but formed the conclusion that Kennedy might be dead and Johnson President. The thought rose like a bubble for just that moment, then it shattered as every one of my senses began to concentrate on the frantic scene that unfolded around me. The death of a President had always been that one ultimate event that lay under the surface in this job of covering Chief Executives. It seemed beyond the possible. Yet, even if buried, it lay explosively in one's mind and only the slightest aberration in the routine was needed to unlock it. Johnson could not have been different. Such a shock might have paralyzed the rationality of a lesser man. It is my judgment that even the white heat of this cruelty did not burn out the Johnson instincts, and that in his crabbed position on the floor of his speeding automobile there was formed, if only almost in the subconscious, a plan to govern if—and there was only one if then—John Kennedy was dead and not just wounded.

From that moment when he sent a Secret Service agent along the sterile tile halls of Parkland Hospital to find out if John Kennedy was really dead, Johnson was in command. His first orders were insignificant, such as assuring protection for his daughters. But, calmly and skillfully, within the next two hours he established total authority. Who knows what forces worked within him? Yet those who watched him sensed two great currents. He was, like everyone else, sickened by the event. But he was still a creature of power. He moved easily and confidently into the void. He even relished it, but only for power's sake, not for John Kennedy's death.

His long experience in the high councils of the government had fitted him perfectly for this sad task. He had without question seen more contemporary history at close range than any other man in the nation. He had seen power shift from Roosevelt to Truman, he had watched the deaths of leaders on the Hill, such as Speaker Sam Rayburn. He had seen men assume command. If Johnson was not an innovator, he was from his

33

years as a legislative leader a superb manager. His life in the Senate had been one of minor crises—such as the 1957 civil-rights bills—and he had sat on the edges of national trauma such as the one when the U2 was shot down over Russia in 1960.

Hold the country together. He pursued that goal with a singlemindedness and skill that no other man in high office could have mustered. He somehow reached out and comprehended that incredible problem, surrounded it and mastered all the details. From ordering the shades on Air Force One drawn, to assembling the apparatus to administer the oath of office, to comforting the Kennedy family, to asking the White House staff to stay with him, to summoning the Cabinet and legislative leaders, and to legions of other matters big and small, Lyndon Johnson worked methodically and knowingly and—in the short view, at least—produced a near-miracle in a storm center of anguish.

Bill Moyers, who flew from Austin to join Johnson on Air Force One, watched the new President as life accelerated beyond calculation. It dawned on Moyers that Johnson was denied the right of a normal human response on that tragic afternoon. The world was in his hands. Uncontrolled emotion in public would be a sign of weakness. Even private grief might be misconstrued in the man who had to lead. Moyers knew that Johnson must feel, as Moyers did, like some instrument of grief thrust harshly into the midst of the deepest human feeling. Moyers grew profoundly proud of Johnson as he watched while the jet raced toward Washington over a stunned nation.

Jack Valenti, who, like Moyers, would be a part of the new government, saw the same things and felt the same way. Once Johnson reached out his hand for a glass of water and Valenti, who was admittedly unsteady, was amazed to see Johnson's fingers extended and steady.

To some, Johnson seemed boorish and unfeeling. They felt that he was grasping for power, somehow rejoicing in the terrible savagery of the day.

The assassination of President Kennedy, it would seem, can only be measured rightly from within its own shock wave. One must know and have known the people who played out the parts—Lyndon Johnson, his Texas cronies, the Irish Mafia of Kennedy. One must be familiar with the usual contradictions of political life, the usual frictions, the incredible complications of Presidential travel. In the vortex of tragedy these increased. That the Kennedy people were stunned and embittered not only at the death of the President but at seeing all he had worked for and stood for pass into the hands of another man is so logical and so natural that the wonder is that Kenny O'Donnell and Larry O'Brien and David Powers and others were so contained and restrained. Those few outbursts, those moments when the resentment showed, when the Kennedy group pulled into itself, were hardly anything to the people there. Only when viewed later from a faraway and unemotional plain did they impress some as inappropriate. The fact of Johnson going about the business of holding the country together, of calling Jackie "Honey" a time or two, of going to Air Force 26000 instead of the back-up plane, of waiting on the ground to take the oath and carry the body of the slain President back—all of this is so reasonable in the context of that day that one wonders how insinuations of inhumanity and great errors of judgment could have arisen. For each action that has been questioned by the critics one could imagine an opposite action that would have brought more criticism. What if Johnson had not gone to Air Force 26000, really the command ship and the one with the crew fully trained for the President? Consider the cries that would have arisen had he not made every effort to be sworn in as soon as possible, or had he not asked the widow of President Kennedy if she wanted to lend her presence to that ceremonial passage of power. It is somehow inconceivable that Jacqueline Kennedy, who had shown an unforeseen depth of courage, would not have wanted the Kennedy presence at the conclusion to the dream, stifling and stark as it was. "Can you imagine," Johnson once asked when the controversy raged, "what would have been said if I, a Texan and the President of the United States, had flown off without Mrs. Kennedy after her husband, the President, had been killed in my state?"

Patient and thoughtful analysis of events and the consideration of alternative actions indicates that LBJ chose in most instances the best course. It has been suggested that because of the strain and tension he was more abrupt, less thoughtful, than he should have been. The opposite is true. In a natural atmosphere he can be, and frequently is, boorish, crude and mean. He was none of those things that day. He was far above his norm in gallantry and consideration. And there is little evidence suggesting that at the time any of the Kennedy people really found him unbearable. Perhaps later, as reason came back, as the full bitterness of the old political feud flamed again and was fanned by despondency, the small mannerisms stood out as affronts. That the Kennedy group on Air Force One flying back to Washington would want to withdraw to themselves, away from Johnson or anybody else on board, is normal reaction. And that somehow they should cling to that camaraderie in going off the airplane, wanting for the moment to exclude the new President, is somehow not very offensive if one can imagine—but, unfortunately, too few can—the emotional atmosphere of the hour.

One stark fact of those hours was the cruelty of the passage of power. That more than anything else has confused the story of Dallas the day of November 22. There is no answer for it. In the split second when Kennedy died the most powerful position that any man has ever held in this world changed hands. The extent of the change was beyond calculation, and in many ways it still is. Millions of lives attached to the Kennedy power structure instantly clouded. National policies as enunciated by John Kennedy simply ceased to exist.

The personal nature of the Presidency was never more clearly demonstrated. The future of business, labor, education had to be recalibrated. The hundreds of Presidential appointees from the embassies around the world to the White House, all of whom had some

37

special bond to John Kennedy, now found themselves faced with a totally new quantity. Communication with the Oval Office stopped, in a sense, and it had to be reopened later. The Chicago *Daily News*'s Peter Lisagor was the first man on the scene to apply the word "cruel" to what everyone had felt but had not quite defined. Lisagor, like others there, had seen that happy band of Kennedyites take over the Democratic party and, one by one, defeat Stuart Symington, Hubert Humphrey, Adlai Stevenson and Lyndon Johnson. He had followed them for three years around the globe as the Kennedy doctrine was enunciated. It had been, by right of hard work and political genius, their government. One small slug of lead had taken it all away as if it had not existed, and had put everything in the hands of the man whom they had fought the hardest in their climb up to the top. Nothing was left for them—not even the machinery of government. Certainly, they could use the airplanes and the communications. But they were borrowing these from Lyndon Johnson, and they knew it.

Those who belonged to the Kennedy inner circle, looking back now, find the change was almost a physical sensation. One moment they rode secure and happy, the possessors of power and the comfortable feeling that they were rightly running this country. In the next moment they were outsiders, almost intruders. There was embarrassment, the sensation of trespassing. Within two hours workmen had begun to remove Kennedy's things from the Oval Office. For those who saw it, that was almost too much to bear. I first saw JFK's possessions being trundled out eight hours later and even then it was a profound shock. There was the urge to put out a hand and stop this madness. But always there was the understanding, even if resented, of the inevitability. It was the United States going on. There was no other way to assure the national life. One death, even the death of the most powerful man on earth, could not, and did not, interfere.

The Kennedy people, buried in grief, had to watch also the shift of attention of the Secret Service, listen to the hospital loudspeaker paging the members of Johnson's staff who would assume their functions. Within two hours LBJ knew intimately the interior of the airplane that had been created by John Kennedy and had been his pride. Johnson had commandeered the phones and the White House photographer. He had plugged himself into the national security apparatus, the Justice Department—indeed, the entire machinery. There was literally nothing else he could do. His responsibility at that moment outweighed that of any other person, and if no one else understood that, he did. Power was his business.

There is no precedent, no government manual, no book of etiquette for an assassination. Men must do what they think best. Lyndon Johnson did that. And perhaps his actions would make a suitable guide for any future Vice President to study. Calls of comfort, like that to Rose Kennedy, mixed with business, like those to McGeorge Bundy. Charles Roberts of *Newsweek,* one of the two reporters who flew back with Air Force One, remembers Johnson's continuing inquiries, relayed through aides, whether the two newsmen had gotten the facts they needed. The other world went on and Johnson did not secede from it.

All sorts of speculation flew through the dark Washington streets. LBJ looked stricken, in shock. His face twitched. He seemed a ghost walking numbly through the rituals of the Presidency. None of it was true. This was the Lyndon Johnson of more than three years earlier—the Lyndon Johnson of the Senate floor, the man with power. His Vice Presidency, as Leonard Baker has written, was an eclipse. There was little of the real Johnson there. By the evening of the 22nd it seemed to many who watched that there had never been a break in his exercise of power. The old instincts were as sharp as ever, many of the old characteristics were reappearing. Bill Moyers was in the outer office of the Vice President's quarters in the Executive Office Building placing calls as he used to do when he was a downy-cheeked Baptist pastor gone pol and guardian of the Majority Leader's outer office on the Hill.

Even now, retracing the major moves and even the trivia of the post-assassination hours, one must marvel at Johnson's total grasp of the machinery of government. He called for a Cabinet meeting the next day. He phoned both former Presidents, Truman and Eisenhower—the older first. He expressed his sorrow to Sargent Shriver, then with hardly a waste motion he phoned FBI Director J. Edgar Hoover and asked for a complete FBI report on the assassination. There was no script for this. For Johnson it was almost reflex.

I wandered across the White House grounds in these hours, trying to comprehend the world that had been ravaged. I looked beyond the fence to the soundless clusters of people, simply standing on the streets staring at the floodlighted White House, at the masses of television cables and machines and men. And I looked up at the brightly lighted windows that were Lyndon Johnson's office and I knew what he was doing. And it was so familiar and so fitting and so necessary and so natural for that man that I had for just a few seconds the sensation that the President had been there all the time and was competently groping now with another national crisis. Crises, whatever they may concern, have familiar birthmarks—communication ganglia, hordes of reporters, lights through the night, mysterious black limousines that glide in and out of the gates, people who gape through the iron bars. All of them were there, and it might have been, except for the terrible wound inside and the immensity of the thing, a Bay of Pigs or Cuban missile crisis. If one had cared about Lyndon Johnson just then or had wanted to watch him closely, there might have been comfort to splintered souls, but most persons pushed him back in their minds. Indeed, it was not until days later that a vast majority of Americans awoke to the fact of his assuredness in the takeover.

On that Friday night Johnson met with his legislative leaders, and in that perhaps more than in anything else lay the real clue to his flawless assumption of power.

The meeting had no real purpose. It was a kind of tribal ritual of those men who wielded the power in the legislative halls. Up on the Hill, meetings are a way of life and a sign of authority. These men understood. Johnson wanted his old friends. He wanted his old forums. He was making them a part of this crisis and at the same time he was becoming part of something new. He was at once establishing his authority and at the same time renewing himself. Hubert Humphrey, who by his nature could feel more deeply than any of the others, lingered behind to give an extra bit of encouragement to his "dear friend." Perhaps when Johnson put his arm around the Senator that night his choice of Vice-Presidential candidate the next year was already made.

Though Johnson was now in command of executive power, vastly different from legislative power—a distinction that LBJ would perhaps never understand— the chemistry of the national crisis was such that it precisely fitted his talents. On the Hill, Johnson was a manager, a consolidator, a consoler, a compromiser. He sought consensus and peace. He wanted harmony beyond results. He was trained to heal a sundered country.

There were no armies to order into the field, nor any complicated diplomatic thickets to transgress. No inspiration was needed from the living President beyond his quiet and reassuring presence. The inspiration for the people was dead and in death was more towering than ever and would grow more so. In a way, it was lucky for

Johnson that the great national sorrow was so heavy that he could not burst onto center stage and posture. He has always lacked terminal facilities. All too frequently he has overdone what he was doing, detracting from his virtuosity, adding unseemliness where none need have been. There were just a few hints that he might have done the same thing then. He was, by Saturday, too eager to move into the Oval Office and to rush the distraught Evelyn Lincoln, personal secretary of John Kennedy, out. He showed his irritation at Bobby Kennedy's tardiness to the Cabinet meeting, imagining odd reasons of vindictiveness rather than the simple and obvious one that Bobby had a smashed heart. But these moments were few. He retreated at just about every hint he might be hurrying things too fast. He stayed in his old office and seemed to realize that he was on the edge of the drama which centered on the flag-draped catafalque in the East Room of the White House. Beyond the legend of the dead Kennedy which was then being magnified in every hamlet was the presence of the Kennedy family. Johnson could not compete with them, nor did he want to. The great and the near-great came in waves for three days. Charles de Gaulle was a more imposing and fascinating figure than the new President. There were Germany's Ludwig Erhard, Queen Frederika, Ireland's marvelous old De Valera and Korea's Chung Hee Park. Mikoyan, Haile Selassie, Diosdado Macapagal. Lyndon Johnson had less glamour than any of them. Thus, awed and overshadowed, stunned into humility and restrained by circumstances, Johnson

43

went quietly about his work of keeping the wheels turning.

The legislative process at which Johnson had so excelled was one of consultation. This was at the heart of the Johnson genius. He saw more people than any other man in the Senate. He quoted Isaiah, "Come now, and let us reason together," constantly, and the many phones in his splendid office, dubbed the Throne Room, were like appendages to his throat. His chamber, a few short steps across the ornate Capitol floors from the Senate cloakroom, was a revolving door for the brotherhood. He met with them over eggs, hamburger and Texas steak. He tippled with them in the evenings and sometimes just stayed there all night when big business was afoot, summoning colleagues, friends, newsmen or anybody else who happened to be moving in the halls at those late hours. His repeatedly successful strategy was to make it appear that the belligerent was winning. He listened patiently to the rantings of the hostile. He had funny Hill Country stories for the glum, and always he made the men in his presence think they were very special, that they had been in the very center of things and their counsel was held in high esteem. It is amazing what this kind of quiet flattery—and special attention to a Senator's political needs—can do. The sharp edges of dissent fade. The voices of doubt tend to grow quiet. Johnson homogenized the Senate. He hated controversy beneath him and around him, and he also disliked divisive views, which he often mistook for anarchy, and so he sought through his endless consulta-

44

tions to make all men think alike, or reasonably so. And when all the necessary work had been done in his office, he strode to the Senate floor, where he conducted the final voting spectacle. It was a splendid sight, this tall man with the canvas face, fingering his inhaler, his mind attuned to every sight and sound and parliamentary nuance. The apparatus was his and he knew each face and every inch of the terrain. Here he was subdued, too, because there was a larger force that he could feel. The men who had made him, such as Georgia's Senator Richard Russell, and those who provided him the horsepower, such as Oklahoma's Bob Kerr, still stared at his back as he signaled the roll calls faster or slower. He stood at his command post, the first seat on the aisle, and he made the legislative business run because through his incessant tinkering he found that adjustment which was just right for a majority and usually more.

It was similar on the weekend of tragedy. His old script worked with few variations. When Johnson stood before the joint session of Congress that Wednesday and said, "All I have ever possessed I would have gladly given not to be here today," he may have been at the summit of both his true popularity and his effectiveness.

SKETCH

HIS HAUNT was the back grounds of the White
House, where the colors of a Washington spring were
breathtaking and the soft evening air cooled and
soothed. He walked with that cowboy gait of his, shoulders lurching from side to side, hands in his pockets,
and he talked, talked, talked. The burdens of war, of
death, of taxes, of disease, of hunger poured out from
Lyndon Johnson. He didn't really ask sympathy, but he
almost pleaded for understanding and sometimes he
nearly demanded it ("There's only one President—
like him or not") from that random band of reporters
and White House staff members who trailed in his wake
as he went around and around the macadam driveway,
nose high in the fresh air, looking off down the South
Lawn toward the Washington Monument and the Jefferson Memorial.

His talk was a safety valve. That valve had to be open
when the pressure mounted. His voice grew hoarse
sometimes from talk and then he had to sip low-cal root
beer to soothe his vocal cords, but on he went. The
sound of his own voice was reassuring. He was thinking
out loud, testing reaction, sculpting concepts, forming
policy.

46

Sometimes he stopped as he went down the drive and the reporters clustered up to him and, like a circuit parson, he raised his arms, doubled his fists and gave them a little scripture. Maybe about how well he and the Congress were doing. He fished in his pockets and pulled out letters. "Here, hold this," he said one night, handing a letter to a reporter so that the man could see the Gettysburg address on the back and nearly perished with curiosity at what Ike had to say to Johnson in that letter. LBJ went slowly through his pocket before he returned to that letter, and then he took it and leisurely read Ike's endorsement of his Vietnam policy.

In the moments when the big issues faded he turned to his yearnings to go to Texas or anything. One time he was reminded of an old Baptist hymn and he walked off looking to the west, with his ragged baritone raised above the shuffle of foot: "Where he leads me, I shall follow. . . . Where he leads me, I shall follow. . . ." He looked up at the big mansion one evening and there was a pause when someone asked how it was to live there. "It's not a home," he said. "It's someplace you go when you finish work. . . . I wake up at five a.m. some mornings and hear the planes coming in at National Airport and I think they are bombing me. . . . There are a thousand conversations going on right under my bedroom with the tourists going through, and I hear every one of them. . . . And when I go up to take a nap in the afternoon, there's Lady Bird and Laurance Rockefeller and eighty women in the next room talking about how the daffodils are doing on Pennsylvania Avenue." He fooled no one with such complaints. He was

47

profoundly happy in the job, and much later when a questioner suddenly asked him, "You love being President, don't you?" he was startled by the directness, but he said, "Yes . . . Yes."

His exuberance often bubbled over, like the time he dragged poet Carl Sandburg from Mansion to Cabinet meeting and then held a press conference from the Truman balcony, shouting to the reporters on the lawn: "Haaaallllloooo down there, I've got Carl Sandburg with me." Or the day at the ranch when he purred: "The cows are fat. The grass is green. The river's full, and the fish are flopping," and then he explained to wide-eyed women correspondents how he once had a bull whose sexual apparatus was askew and the poor beast kept missing the mark, whereupon he jumped in his Lincoln and burned up some Texas highways at near ninety miles per hour, passing on a hill and forcing an oncoming car to the shoulder, while gleefully shielding the speedometer with his hat. It was his kind of paean to the Presidency in those first days.

VISION

THE TERM "Great Society" had an inauspicious birth. It simply appeared on the page in Richard N. Goodwin's small Smith-Corona typewriter on a chill night in early March of 1964. It was near midnight, and the rumpled Goodwin, then the Secretary General of the International Peace Corps Secretariat, was as usual puffing his way through a collection of large cigars in one of those government-issue offices with steel desks, steel chairs and bleak walls on Washington's Connecticut Avenue. Presidential speechwriters seem, for some undetermined reason, to function best in the very early hours when most of Washington has gone to bed. Goodwin was not then what could be called a full-fledged Presidential speechwriter. He had not moved to the White House. He was operating secretly on special writing tasks under the direction of Johnson's Special Assistant Bill Moyers, who had been deputy director of the Peace Corps. On that March night he was responding to a Presidential request relayed in the tepid waters of the White House swimming pool. Moyers, Goodwin and some other aides had joined Johnson in his afternoon exercise period, which, as usual, after a few perfunctory struggles in the water, dissolved into a moist and relaxed discussion of Presidential matters. On that March afternoon Johnson was feeling good about his Presidency. He had passed the $11.5-billion tax cut which Kennedy had espoused. He was winning the Kennedy civil-rights bill, the strongest legislation of its kind in a hundred years. In short, the Kennedy days were over— the President had fulfilled his obligation to the New Frontier. It was now time, Johnson told his listeners, for the Johnson Administration to be initiated, and he wanted some bold new national directions. He told his men to think about how and when he should tell the country that he was ready to take the next step forward. In a few days Johnson was scheduled to make the presentation of the first Eleanor Roosevelt memorial award to Anna M. Kross, a New York judge. After more thought and conversation about the new national emphasis, Moyers asked Goodwin to prepare a speech for the Kross award ceremony which would begin to chart the new course.

Goodwin's charter was vague. Those things always are. They are feelings more than directives. Especially with Lyndon Johnson, whose great energies and desires even he is sometimes at a loss to explain. The impulse to move ahead was strong in Johnson. It always had been. Inside that hulking frame was the venturesome heart of a prairie Populist. He believed in change. He was a disciple of the doctrine that you had to keep reaching, struggling. If you didn't move, you lost out. "I want every tenant farmer's child to have a chance to do what men like John Sparkman and I have done. That's the thing that will keep this system surviving," he said. In Johnson's world very little was stationary or permanent. Men died. Rivers flooded. Drouth came. Banks foreclosed. Men grew rich. Cities boomed. Towns shriveled. A political system had to enfold that endless horizon and adjust to all the variations in the landscape and try somehow to gently—yes, gently, that was important to LBJ—bring more order and more equity, all the time prodding and preaching and progressing. Johnson's life was like that. Restless, spasmodic, tumultuous. After a cold winter's day of back-breaking labor on the road gang he went off to college. When he found the teachers of his small school in Cotulla spending the recess time smoking in the boiler room, he ordered them out to organize and supervise the kids' play, and when the complaints came to the school board, the board suggested pointedly that what it ought to do was fire the other teachers and hire more like Lyndon Johnson. He went into politics to find the world. He proposed to Lady Bird after a one-week courtship, later plunged her inherited money into a radio station, a dubious business in a dubious time. He stood behind Franklin Roosevelt when others were deserting him and won a seat in Congress and a friend who would open the world to him. He campaigned for the Senate in one of the first helicopters ever seen in Texas, halloooing down his political buncombe through a bullhorn from that flailing, rickety apparition called *The Johnson City Windmill.* He was always ahead, always thrusting beyond the comfortable limits. He was a paradox, of course. He didn't want to let people know he was an insurgent. "The country wants to be comfortable," he told historian Arthur Schlesinger, Jr., in 1960. "It doesn't want to be stirred up. Have a revolution, all right, but don't say anything about it until you are entrenched in office. That's the way Roosevelt did it." Well, maybe not, but Johnson was always imprecise. He didn't want trouble, yet he wanted revolution. That strange dichotomy would get him into a lot of difficulty as President. Still, it worked on the way up. ("It takes a carpenter to build a barn, but any jackass can kick one down.")

In the first months of his Presidency, in a great burst of talk and press-agentry, he gouged out some very rough lines of action. The core of his early message came when he reported somberly in January to Congress on the State of the Union.

"Let this session of Congress be known as the session which did more for civil rights than the last hundred sessions combined; as the session which enacted the most far-reaching tax cut of our time; as the session which declared all-out war on human poverty and unemployment in these United States; as the session which finally recognized the health needs of all our older citizens; as the session which reformed our tangled transportation and transit policies; as the session which achieved the most effective, efficient foreign-aid program ever; and as the session which helped build more homes, more schools, more libraries, and more hospitals than any single session of Congress in the history of our Republic." This was vintage Johnson. It was a program that the old hands called "a laundry list"—there was everything in it. It was Johnson, too, in that it was simply a call for more, still an extension of the quantitative programs begun by Franklin Roosevelt. Johnson was then in a half-world, struggling to emerge from his past and that of Kennedy into a future of his own devising.

Johnson was haunted by the Great Depression—the invisible scar, author Caroline Bird called it—and he declared a war on waste. It was another call from the past, admonishing everyone to clean their plates, turn out the lights, patch up their clothes. He lined up some Internal Revenue Service officers and laid out, in his singular style, his ideas. "You don't have to be wasteful to be enlightened or to be progressive. My mother was the most liberal person that I think I ever knew. Yet she always had some pin money hidden under the pillow to take care of our needs in time of distress. I think we must have a war on poverty, but we must have a war on waste." There was a certain wisdom in resurrecting frugality as a national theme. The Congress was in a mood for it, being on the edge of trauma over the prospect of a national budget that seemed destined to break the $100-billion barrier. In fact, Virginia's crusty Senator Harry Byrd, chairman of the Finance Committee, won from Johnson a budget below $100 billion in exchange for a promise to vote for the tax cut. Johnson was wildly contradictory, however, in thrashing around for a position of his own. While pledged to save, he promised more. "I want a home for every American," he said one evening to a visitor, thumping him on the knee. Then he added casually, "We're going to clean up the slums, too."

These domestic doctrines were delivered everywhere and anywhere in the early months. Johnson roamed the back yard of the White House, summoned the press to his desk and his den, talked over the dinner table to individual callers. "Aside from being solvent," Johnson said to one group, "this country's government must always be compassionate." He called the new immigration bill "a matter of common sense and common decency." On Lincoln's birthday, before the great statue in the Memorial, the President said that Lincoln's work would be unfulfilled "so long as there are any Americans of any race or color who are denied their full human rights—so long as there are any Americans of any place or region who are denied their human dignity." These thoughts and more flowed from Johnson in early 1964. At times they almost overwhelmed the people, they came in such a floodtide.

Something was in Johnson's heart. But it was not yet in his mind. He needed someone to think out a road map for him and supply the symbols and the language. Dick Goodwin puffed away at his cigars, and there it was at the end of a chain of thought—the "great society." The New Deal was ending. The problems of want were now becoming the lesser problems of national life. The problems of affluence were concerning more people. Thus, in Goodwin's imagery, what we had to do was move beyond a rich and powerful society to a "great society." He plunked the keys of his little typewriter methodically, feeling good about the slogan but not really understanding just then that he had labeled the Johnson Administration. The speech draft was dutifully placed before Moyers the next day, and he in turn passed it along to Jack Valenti, who was then the chief editor. Goodwin's creation there came to the end of its short life. Valenti felt that for the Eleanor Roosevelt award, Johnson should talk about the role of women in government, and so the Goodwin draft was shelved. (Had Eleanor Roosevelt been around, she would have been appalled to learn that what she had inspired was not to be used in her memory, and that instead she was to be eulogized with such lines as "I am unabashedly in favor of women.")

Johnson did not forget Goodwin's great society. Before he adopted it, however, he circled it warily. In an interview with the television networks he said he had not thought of a slogan, "but I suppose all of us want a better deal, don't we?" That got a journalistic tryout for a few days, but faded rapidly. In April, talking to editors and broadcasters in the Rose Garden, he urged developing a "greater society." A couple of days later he jetted to Chicago for a fund-raising dinner sponsored by the Democratic Club of Cook County, and there he warmly squeezed the arm of Mayor Richard Daley ("my old and trusted friend"), peered through the smoky chasm of McCormick Place and bellowed, "We have been called upon to build a great society of the highest order." His jolly crowd was not paying enough attention. The President paused, looked down sternly. "We have been called upon—are you listening?—to build a great society of the highest order, a society not just for today or tomorrow, but for three or four generations to come." Several more times that evening he used the words, although still not like a slogan. Back in Washington, Goodwin, very wise in the ways of bureaucracy, began to dispatch memos to Johnson urging that Great Society become the slogan of the new movement. In more than a dozen speeches over the next month the President used the symbol, although still with no formal recognition of it as the banner of the Administration. Within the White House, Moyers and Valenti liked it, Horace Busby had mild reservations. That hardly mattered. Lyndon Johnson had seized on it and, what was more important, he had seized on Dick Goodwin, one of the most remarkable thirty-two-year-olds to work in Washington in three decades. Before he finally left the Johnson Administration at the close of 1965, Goodwin almost more than anyone else in the White House was responsible for taking the raw emotion of Lyndon Johnson and sculpting it into the graceful and promising lines of the Great Society that so moved the nation. Goodwin almost singlehandedly provided the scripts for the most inspiring moments of Johnson's first two years. The absence of elevating rhetoric in the following two years had a profound effect on the political fortunes of Lyndon Johnson.

Goodwin was one of those comets which come through the national government from decade to decade. They are rare. They sometimes produce more of a spectacle than a lasting impact, but while they burn they light the dark corners. His was certainly the most facile and remarkable mind in government under both Kennedy and Johnson. He had led his classes at Tufts and Harvard Law School. He had clerked under Supreme Court Justice Felix Frankfurter and then served as an investigator in the television quiz-show inquiry conducted by Congressman Oren Harris. He joined the Kennedy campaign as a speechwriter in 1959 and became a member of the happy White House crew in the New Frontier. He was too impatient and too abrasive to stand still. Skeptic, iconoclast, professional irritant, he won friends and enemies in about the same proportion and with equally high devotion. Goodwin devised the concept of the Alliance for Progress, one of Kennedy's shining programs in the early months of the New Frontier. As one of Kennedy's special Latin American operatives, Goodwin soon ruffled enough career men to be moved to the State Department, where he continued to eschew musty diplomatic doctrine and walk on official toes. Throughout all his exile, which next led to the International Peace Corps Secretariat, Kennedy never lost track of him nor ever lost interest in his mental mechanism. JFK frequently called Goodwin just to talk a problem over. On the day Kennedy was murdered—

indeed, at the very moment he got the news—Goodwin was in his home typing out a Presidential statement for release the next day announcing that he was returning to the White House as the President's special assistant on the arts. That appointment, of course, vanished with Dallas. Goodwin promptly wrote to Johnson absolving him of any obligation and then went back to his austere Peace Corps office, his future uncertain.

On a day in late January he went to the White House with Peace Corps Chief Sargent Shriver to address an assemblage of intellectuals. Johnson caught sight of Goodwin in a back corridor and beckoned him to his side. "Come on in the office a minute," he told Goodwin, and there he explained his problem with the Panama uprising. He needed a Presidential statement. He had a draft of a statement from the State Department, but he was not happy with it, the President told Goodwin. It was too truculent. What would he suggest? asked Johnson. Goodwin said he felt that the proper United States position was one of tolerance. Panama was a tiny country and it behooved us just to be nice. "Do you want me to write something?" Goodwin asked. Johnson said he did. Goodwin soon produced a statement, which was sent to the White House, and then there was silence. After three days Johnson suddenly appeared on television and read the Goodwin statement verbatim. From then on Goodwin was marked as a man Johnson wanted. But the President was hyperconscious about his staff appointments. He was still laboring under the illusion that the American people believed their Presidents wrote their own speeches. Goodwin began to get secret assignments.

The urge to declare the Great Society in a serious and detailed speech grew with Johnson. He talked it over with his aides, who looked ahead at the appointments schedule. Everyone was in agreement that such a declaration should be made on a campus. Johnson had a commitment to give the University of Michigan's commencement address in May, and that was selected for the launching of the Great Society.

As was so often the case in Johnson's government, there were parallel efforts to draft this charter. Busby and Valenti formed an unofficial team that favored a more moderate declaration of purpose. The young revolutionary Goodwin went to work under the hand of Bill Moyers, who was then twenty-nine, to put into words Johnson's feelings and his own. For the moment, at least, what was on Goodwin's mind was almost more important than what the President had been brooding about.

To Goodwin the Great Society was the distillation of a long and deep thought process that had been going on since the day he had set foot in Washington six years earlier. The nation, as Goodwin later recalled, had been straining to give some shape to its domestic future. The war had arrested the creative energies of the New Deal. By the time the war was over, an era had passed and it was time for a new national philosophy, for new forms of government. Yet the archaic structures of the New Deal lived on. So did the thought and the language, while the country involved itself in the postwar world trauma and its own immense productive jag created by the long war. Dwight Eisenhower's years were a quiet time of breath-catching, and then there came a wave of doubt about our national purpose as domestic prosperity went beyond imagination and the world settled down to relative peace. Thoughtful people such as Time Inc.'s Henry Luce felt that the United States must turn to the pursuit of excellence in its life. Kennedy adopted that as one of his campaign calls. There was under President Kennedy a marked shift in emphasis from sheer quantity to the quality of our national life.

Goodwin's job was one of definition: to explain this national hunger and, in a broad way, outline Lyndon Johnson's very large feeling about what should be done. It is almost impossible to overemphasize the importance of rhetoric in today's Presidency—rhetoric, that is, in its largest sense, embracing thought and sincerity and substance. The unavoidable daily electronic involvement with as many as ninety million Americans means that a Presidential sentence may have more impact than an entire speech of fifty years ago. There is no way to measure such things, but language may be the most important tool that a President has for governing this sprawling nation. John Kennedy alerted the people to himself through his skill in expression. In a listless period his words brought a new sense of self-confidence, of dignity, of uplift. The Kennedy rhetoric set a tone in Washington that attracted superior men and women to the government. Eloquence won new global prestige. True, none of Kennedy's superb entreaties won over the cold hearts of Congress. But hindsight suggests to me that the country liked what it heard and was far ahead of the politicians. Certainly Kennedy's exposition of new economics provided the national enlightenment and thence the momentum that made passage of the tax cut an inevitability. "Presidential power is the power to persuade," claims Richard Neustadt, director of the Kennedy Institute for Politics and a close student of the Presidency. The next step, if that is true, is how it is done. "The most eminent presidents have generally been eloquent presidents," writes Stanford's Thomas A. Bailey in his book *Presidential Greatness.* "They are eloquent with pen, as Jefferson was; or with tongue, as Franklin Roosevelt was; or with both, as Wilson and Lincoln were." The "feeling" about a President is determined in large measure by how he talks and what he talks about. And in turn his program is also so measured. The speechwriting process forces the formulation of policy. In the intense concentration that a Presidential address requires, new ideas are frequently forged and emerge on the page of the writer. In the longer view, Presidential speeches are the signposts of history.

Goodwin cast out the enormous governmental net for the best thinking from every department. The memos flowed into his new office, a large unmarked chamber in the Executive Office Building across from the White House Executive Wing. He had been moved for convenience but not for identity yet. Goodwin talked more with the President and he studied the material before him. The New Deal, as Goodwin reasoned at his typewriter, had been dedicated to raising living standards, to abolishing the problems of want. That war now had been largely won. Certainly a final national effort was needed to complete the unfinished business that Roosevelt had started. But now 82 percent of the families had annual incomes above $3,000. The question which Goodwin then addressed himself to was the kind of life which the majority of the United States citizens were leading. It was obvious that, in many sectors of our national life, quality was deteriorating as income went up. Private wealth was not curing public ills. The landscape that the people viewed was too often either monotonous or scarred. On 265,000 miles of interstate and primary highways surveyed, 17,762 highly visible junkyards were counted along the sides. The air the people breathed was dirty and getting dirtier. In Los Angeles, the smog capital, 13,730 tons of contaminants were released into the atmosphere every day, most of it from the 3.75 million automobiles. By 1980 the auto population of that city alone was expected to be nearly 6 million. Water was filling up with sewage and industrial waste. One fourth of Lake Erie, for example, was too polluted to support marine life. Education, too, was often in turmoil, the quality not improving. In depressed areas children fell far below the national norm. In Appalachia 30 percent failed the Selective Service Educational Tests. Cores of cities were rotting as the affluent fled to the suburbs only to buy homes in neighborhoods unimaginatively set down on treeless plains. The great economic machine that American ingenuity had created was working at odds with human needs, and we were in a very critical hour. "What good did it do," said Goodwin later, "to own two cars if the highways were jammed and the parks overflowing? What good was leisure time if what you said and heard and were able to do was of no consequence? What good were all the medical advances if the air you breathed and the water you drank was not healthy? What was our prosperity all about?"

Not all of Goodwin's ideas could be included in the text because of length. He had to abandon a section dealing with governmental reform, the call for new working relationships between all levels of government. The premise was that the private sector of the nation had to change to survive—competition simply eliminated the inefficient. But government had no such cleansing agent. Roosevelt had devised new institutions to handle his innovations. There had been no change since then. The current problems were being processed through thirty-year-old systems. All the old failures were carried along. But such thoughts had to wait for a later day.

Those were exciting hours for Goodwin and Moyers. To simply talk about one's dreams for a more perfect society is pleasurable. To be in a position actually to influence the national direction was a heady experience. The text that Goodwin finally produced was rooted in Lyndon Johnson's restless soul. There was the influence of Moyers, a very worldly but youthful man, and then there were the energy and grace of Goodwin's intellect. Indeed, the only lines in the finished speech which came from outside the White House were suggested by the Interior Department's James Reston, a son of *The New York Times*'s Reston. "A few years ago we were greatly concerned about the 'Ugly American.' Today we must act to prevent an ugly America." The language in Goodwin's document was superb, the vision even better. He had hit upon an alliterative device that pleased Johnson greatly—the three C's: "So I want to talk to you today about three places where we begin to build the Great Society—in our cities, in our countryside, and in our classrooms."

Johnson was instantly enchanted with the text. He brushed aside a more conservative draft done by other aides. There was a close call for the Ann Arbor speech. LBJ had by then imposed Jack Valenti between himself and his creative people. Valenti was billed as the master editor, the man who focused all of the written efforts of the White House and edited them before they went to the President. He pursued the great books in his bathtub, where he had had a reading rack installed, and in spare moments at his desk (Macaulay, Burke, Durant, Toynbee), but his personal style sprang from his more flamboyant days as a Houston public-relations counselor and advertising executive, and it was frequently in conflict with the more significant and dignified prose required in the affairs of state. Valenti edited out the heart of the Goodwin premise. When Goodwin saw what had happened, he rushed to the office of Moyers, who agreed that the penciling had damaged the speech, and the two went to Johnson, who liked the original version. ("He can't write an English sentence," McGeorge Bundy was said to have commented once about Johnson, "but he is a hell of a good editor.") One measure of Jack Valenti was that he learned from mistakes rather than becoming embittered. He became one of the strongest advocates of the Great Society as pronounced finally on May 22 in Ann Arbor. There was some quiet background opposition to the Goodwin approach, however. Horace Busby, one of those who wanted a more moderate mantle for Johnson's Administration, lobbied at low key against the Goodwin effort. Busby's reservations concerned the future. The Great Society as outlined by Goodwin was a towering thought, a concept of such magnificent self-confidence that Busby feared it might smack of arrogance. That happened to be Johnson's state of mind in the spring of 1964, however. He had held the nation together in its grief over Kennedy, a country that in three years had erased its missile-gap fears, faced down Khrushchev in Cuba, eased the cold war and created an expansive economy that had shattered every previous high. Why not a Great Society?

It was hot that day in May in Ann Arbor. The sweating press corps shucked their suit coats and talked more about the great football legends established by All-American Tom Harmon, who had once played in the stadium where Johnson was to deliver his speech. The President arrived—big, dripping, but inspired. He lifted his country.

"For a century we labored to settle and to subdue a continent. For half a century we called upon unbounded invention and untiring industry to create an order of plenty for all of our people.

"The challenge of the next half-century is whether we have the wisdom to use that wealth to enrich and elevate our national life, and to advance the quality of our American civilization.

"Your imagination, your initiative, and your indignation will determine whether we build a society where progress is the servant of our needs, or a society where old values and new visions are buried under unbridled growth. For in your time we have the opportunity to move not only toward the rich society and the powerful society, but upward to the Great Society.

"The Great Society is a place where every child can find knowledge to enrich his mind and to enlarge his talents. It is a place where leisure is a welcome chance to build and reflect, not a feared cause of boredom and restlessness. It is a place where the city of man serves not only the needs of the body and the demands of commerce but the desire for beauty and the hunger for community.

"It is a place where man can renew contact with nature. It is a place which honors creation for its own sake and for what it adds to the understanding of the race. It is a place where men are more concerned with the quality of their goals than the quantity of their goods."

VIGNETTE

THE BIG DAY came with cold, but there was sunshine. It crept up over the white Capitol dome, flooded down the salted expanse of Pennsylvania Avenue and gradually wakened the city.

Lyndon Johnson was up at 6:40 and although the White House was bulging with cousins and aunts, he and Lady Bird ate breakfast alone in the mansion. Beside him was his inaugural address. Virtually every spare minute for days past had been devoted to its prose. And after the quiet breakfast he worked on it still more, reading it, changing a word here and there, worrying about it because this was the time he was going to become President in his own right.

At 11:15 all was ready. The glistening black limousines were lined up in front of the White House. The President, the Vice President, their wives and families, the escorts—Senator Everett Jordan and Speaker John McCormack—had all sipped their coffee and were ready. The sound system along Pennsylvania Avenue was emitting the strains of "We're in the Money" as the caravan began to glide down the White House drive.

The wedge of motorcycle police sped up the avenue.

67

Johnson walked quickly into the Capitol beneath the rotunda. He smoothed his clothing, put in his contact lenses. Then, suddenly, the notes of "Hail to the Chief" sounded for Johnson, the President that was and the President to be—almost two different people, for on this day there was to be a new beginning. He took small, quick steps in a way that was unnatural to him. He was a man trying not to appear cocky or powerful.

The scene was both beautiful and significant, one of those vignettes that say what this country is all about. Poignant with memory. Exhilarating with hope. The sun was warm, filtered only by a gauze of clouds. The Capitol shone, and below was the crowd in winter reds, blues and greens. George Washington cast a stony gaze over the scene from his place above the Capitol door. People festooned the old building itself. They were on the stairs, behind the pillars, looking out the windows. The Johnson informality was noticeable. There were no top hats or tails or even morning coats. The sun began to melt the snow on the roof of the inaugural portico and the drops splattered on the shoulders of Congressmen Hale Boggs and Emanuel Celler.

This was a beginning, yet many could not help a backward glance, and for the time it lasted there was a cutting sorrow about what had once been and could be no longer. One had to look hard to find the Kennedy faces. Sargent and Eunice Shriver were almost lost among Texans. Teddy Kennedy kept his head down. Bobby thrust his chin up, but it was hard for him.

The President's time came. He rose ponderously

from his chair. Lady Bird took four steps and stood at his left. She held the old family Bible. Then Chief Justice Earl Warren began the thirty-six seconds that were so important to Lyndon Johnson and the world.

CONSENSUS

C o n s e n s u s?" said Johnson one night, weighing
the term, not sure whether he could really deny it,
not sure whether he wanted to, but obviously not liking
it. Then suddenly he made up his mind. "That's not
mine. That's Walter Lippmann's word." He was right.
It was not his term. But it was his technique for governing—at least in the first two years.

It was the way to bring about the revolution he
wanted without anybody realizing it until it was on
them. It was his Senate device, relentlessly applied. It
was even deeper than that—he simply wanted everybody to be friendly and do what he wanted; then he
would be happy and so would they, or at least he
thought so. "I want to avoid any implication that I'm
slappin' or rappin' at anyone," he said one day. "I've
done everything I could to avoid conflict, to avoid increasing tension, to avoid harassing. I try to avoid all
that, just as I try to avoid saying ugly things about
labor, industry, the farmer, any group in this country."

In his quest for consensus, Johnson invoked Isaiah

frequently and he had an incurable urge to plead for unity as if it were a national religion. "I have two favorite speeches," he told reporters on his 1964 campaign jet. "The one I gave in New Orleans, and . . . and . . ." The President paused and looked at Press Secretary Reedy. "What was that other one day before yesterday when I was healin' the wounds again, George?"

Finally, there was just a yearning for plain old affection. A loner and a fighter most of his life, he had a deep void within him. "The most stimulating thing in my kind of work is the feeling that the people care about me," he told one Rose Garden group, which he then led into his office to view slides of himself shaking hands with hordes of campaign cheerers. After a few jubilant frames, projected under the guidance of Valenti, Johnson chortled, "I'm sure glad we got rid of that image that nobody likes Lyndon." Turning to Valenti, he asked, "Got any more [slides]?"

Down there inside of Johnson somewhere was an image of a great popular leader something like Franklin Roosevelt, except more so, striding over the land and cupping the people in his hands and molding a national unity that every President dreams about but none is ever able to achieve. Johnson's ambitions, of course, were bigger than any other President's.

Lack of that unity had bothered him during the New Frontier, although he had said little about it until it was all over. "We [the New Frontier] were wrong with the country. A lot of people thought we were rapping on doors at midnight. There was the steel business. There was a row about the FBI interviewing Barry Goldwater at dawn. Actually, Bobby Kennedy had called him and Barry said please send them at seven o'clock in the morning, but it was at his request because he was leaving early. . . . The whole Administration was pretty much misunderstood. Kennedy was not anti-business or radical, as he was sometimes portrayed. I was portrayed as 'ineffectual' or a 'Throttlebottom.' "

And in almost everything he said in those first days, his great hunger for togetherness came out. "I try to carry forward with a minimum of vituperation and ugly exchanges . . . telling a man to go to hell and making him go to hell are two different propositions." Johnson learned a lot from FDR, but he never believed in provoking the opposition as his old mentor had done. "Other Presidents," LBJ said one day, "have gotten people sore, have called them 'economic royalists' and things like that, then they lost the support of the people like the President of ITT and John Lewis. I try to get everything out of them. I try to bleed these folks. Why, I can learn more from a lunch with Arthur Krock than from a book, he's been around much longer than I have. Success is based on working together. It doesn't follow that the head of the U.S. Rubber Company and the head of the rubber workers' union can't like each other. I'd rather have them spend six days working together than six months on strike."

The President was consistent. Not only did he preach this brotherhood doctrine for the nation, but he suggested it would work in the world as well. "I try to do what a baseball player does when he sees a high fast ball coming at him—he steps out of the box for a moment and lets it go by. I treat Harold Wilson just as I'd like to be treated. If De Gaulle wants to come to Washington and talk, I'll treat him that way too. We'll get along better then and I hope something good will come of it."

He wanted the rogues to come along with him, too. In the midst of some of Alabama's racial troubles, Governor George Wallace flew to Washington to ask for Federal aid, and in his hearing before the President, Johnson loomed over him and implored, "When you're gone, George, don't you want your people to build a great, big, white, marble monument with the inscription 'George Wallace, He Built' on it, or do you want them to leave a little, tiny, scrawny pine shingle with 'George Wallace, He Hated' written on it?"

Kennedy's death provided precisely the national frame of mind in which Johnson's unity theories could be put to work effectively. And just when consensus might have begun to fragment of natural causes, along came candidate Barry Goldwater, who frightened the doubtful back to the President's side. Johnson's own managerial skill—keeping consensus was essentially a manager's job—carried effective consensus until 1965, when it at last began to fragment badly because of the commitment made that summer to fight in Vietnam and because of Johnson's failure of communication. Within those two years, however, the legislative achievements were without parallel, proving to Johnson

73

the unifier that his Senate technique could be used in the White House. It was illusory after 1965, though Johnson clung to his familiar routine up until the winter of 1967, when his Gallup rating had fallen to 38 percent. Then he began to show leadership in the more traditional sense, responding to critics bluntly and taking unpopular but necessary positions more openly. Yet he did even that reluctantly.

Essential to Johnson's managerial technique was man-to-man persuasion. It had been his forte in the Senate and, in fact, the only way to operate tellingly in that secretive atmosphere. Johnson could not persuade effectively on a broad front. His Senate speeches were unmoving. His 1960 effort to capture the Democratic nomination had proved his almost total inability to reach out for support beyond his legislative world. But with a country unified by tragedy, Johnson discovered in the first week he was President that applying his devices to the leaders who gathered in Washington strengthened his base immeasurably.

Proof that his "treatment," as it was called, from his old Senate days had a place in the executive life was given to Johnson by his success in the first year in preventing a nationwide rail strike. "A fellow from Texas said to me that he'd listened for four years of debate and negotiation and he'd had enough. Then he got up and went to the bathroom. When he came back I said: 'You're from Dallas and you gave President Kennedy, a fellow from New England, three and a half years in which to try to settle this strike and you won't give me three weeks. Is that fair?' He said, 'Can you get by on two weeks?' And I said, 'Yes,' and I got it." Lyndon Johnson put the carriers and the unions in a room in the Executive Office Building across from the White House and he kept them there. The power of the Presidency was all about them. The country was gazing at them. There was almost nothing else the participants could do but settle their differences. Johnson knew that. He preached a little of his Texas wisdom. "You represent the unions. You know more about what your men need than anybody else in the country. You represent the industry and you know more about what the railroads can do than any other man. Now, if I were either of you, I sure as hell would want to get in there and settle that strike before somebody like Lyndon Johnson, who doesn't know much about either side, has to do it." There was a certain cogency to the President's simple wisdom. The nation, which had grown used to unresolved labor issues, was startled when a settlement came. Johnson was quietly jubilant. "Lady Bird was standing by the elevator in the living quarters and she looked little and woebegone until—I knew nobody could see me—I gave her this sign [circled fingers]. But then I thought I was wrong. One of the railroad executives from the Chicago road started out by saying, 'I'm just an old country boy—' And I cut him off by saying: 'When I hear that I put my hand on my billfold; don't start that with me.' He replied by saying, 'By God, all I was going to say was that I'm ready to sign up.' That broke the deadlock. You can be wrong about people;

I'll never know what he was going to say when I broke in. . . . I wonder."

Such triumphs made the Johnson juices boil. A spectacle was demanded so that the country could share in his success. LBJ wanted to make the announcement on television, and since the agreement had come in the afternoon, he wanted it on the prime evening news times, which he knew down to the minute. He called in the TV experts and told them he wanted to hit the American screens about seven p.m. The elaborate TV studio in the White House had not yet been built, so it was decided that Johnson would race to the CBS studio four miles away. The President's limousine was hurried around in back of the White House. He loped out, followed by Labor Secretary Willard Wirtz, Roy Davidson of the union, J. E. Wolfe of the carriers, and assorted others who always seemed to trail him in a mysterious cloud. All of them jammed into the black car and it shot out of the southwest gate of the White House going so fast it passed four motorcycle officers who were stationed there to provide escort to the studio. I recall dashing madly for my car with *The New York Times*'s Tom Wicker. We tried desperately to keep up with the President, who was weaving through rush-hour traffic at fifty to sixty miles per hour, but it was futile.

When we arrived at the studio, Johnson was stationed before the cameras with Wolfe and Davidson. "Let's go, let's go," he urged. He did not want to miss the Huntley-Brinkley show, which was just then ending. He had it calculated precisely. Just as a puffing Secret

Service man hung the Presidential seal on the podium, Johnson stepped up, Wirtz and others behind him, Wolfe and Davidson seated at his sides. It was to be family-style. "Let's go," he rasped in irritation. "Let's get on before seven." Then Johnson was on the air—the national impresario. He introduced Secretary Wirtz and Davidson and Wolfe, in what seemed a kind of governmental Lawrence Welk show, hovering over the smaller men as they read their parts. Johnson read the now famous letter from little Cathy May Baker in Chicago, who was fearful that her grandmother would not be able to come visit her—a soap-opera touch. Now Cathy's grandmother could ride the train. When he finished, the President folded up Cathy's letter and very neatly placed it in his pocket. He led his contingent out of the studio in quest of the nearest TV set, saying, "What I want to see is how they handle it on the seven-p.m. Cronkite show." Corny as the performance was, it was still heady fare to the participants. Wolfe and Davidson had been exposed to an elemental force which they had never encountered before. They were pleasantly swept along. In the tiny studio elevator they pressed up to each other, these antagonists, then they noticed it and both grinned self-consciously. "Now we are friends again," said Wolfe. "Why, we've never been enemies," answered Davidson. He clapped Wolfe on the shoulder and they walked out of the studio like brothers. Such was the magic of Lyndon Johnson's personal touch.

He was like a great maestro when he exercised the

technique, modulating and adjusting to every situation. When he had Germany's Chancellor Ludwig Erhard in his car at the ranch and they were driving out to see the deer play at dusk in the hills, the President got stern, poked his guest on the knee and suggested that the Germans quit worrying about United States support so much—they had it; what they should worry about was helping out more in the underdeveloped regions of the world. He had the same hard edge for Canada's Lester Pearson, who came to lunch with Johnson at Camp David in 1965 after making a speech in Cleveland in which he urged a bombing pause. A miffed Johnson looked across at Pearson. "What would you do," he asked Pearson, "disarm without them doing it?" Pearson answered, "Oh, no." And then Johnson bored in. "Well, why didn't you mention them in your speech?" Pearson was a more humble man throughout the meal.

The script was replayed in another dazzling affair— the steel-industry settlement in the fall of 1965. He appealed to patriotism and good sense. "You know about wages and profits," he told I. W. Abel of the steelworkers and R. Conrad Cooper of the steel industry, "but I know about this nation's position in the world, and I'm saying to you that neither will be served by your being hard-headed. . . . When the great captains of the steel industry say, 'We're not going to reopen the question' and when the mighty steelworkers answer, 'This far and no more,' then you are saying to our men in Vietnam, 'We're behind you most of the way, but of course you've got to take into account that we have special problems.' " He reminded the negotiators, whom he put into the Executive Office Building for five days and nights, that they should not let the 1959 strike be repeated. "Don't let that happen again. Split up that loss and give it in pensions and wages and profits." Johnson had jokes as the negotiations went through a long week. "Tell them," he instructed his aides, "that Mrs. Johnson is calling and asking who is going to pay for that board bill over there." And then one morning Joe Califano called the President at his desk and said, "Mr. President, we've got them in agreement." Lyndon Johnson answered, "The hell you say." For a few fleeting hours Johnson was king again.

He used a few threats, but not so many as some suggested. He twisted arms, but not so much as was often thought. There was a great deal of truth in Johnson's own explanation of his devices: "You've got to reason these things out together. Why, I read in the paper that those governors out there in the Midwest were opposed to Vietnam and I got on the phone and I sent the airplane out for them and I told them to get back here so I could talk to them. . . . People say that I twist Congressmen's arms and make deals with them. . . . They come down here and we talk things out and I tell them what's good for the country and they understand and they go back and that's the way things work around here."

He was tough when aluminum producers raised prices. He ordered stockpiled aluminum released to batter back the increase, and he let his anger be known.

"Those aluminum producers were acting like profit-eers," he raged to one of his men. "They were making record profits. How much do they want? They said they wouldn't smelt it [stockpile]. Well, I'm the Commander-in-Chief and I can go out and get it smelted." Such harsh words were rare with Johnson. On one notable occasion they failed totally. When Bob Kennedy came back from Europe in 1967 and went to the White House to report on his observations and to clear up the false story that he had gotten a peace feeler, Johnson read the somber assessment as an indictment of his foreign policy. He jumped on Kennedy, accusing him of contriving the peace-feeler incident, of "tying our boys' hands behind their backs." The President added, "If you keep talking like this, you won't have a political future in this country within six months." Rather than subduing Kennedy, this onslaught merely enraged him, and the Johnson-Kennedy bitterness deepened—something that Johnson could afford less than Kennedy at the time.

He sometimes was rather sad when he didn't win over the opposition, or when others accused him of not consulting them enough. Ev Dirksen issued such a complaint, and Johnson quickly went to his Senate friend. "Now, why did you say that, Everett?" Johnson wanted to know. "Well, Mr. President," answered Dirksen, "you must remember I am the leader of your loyal opposition. And when three dogs come at you, you have to feed them some hamburger." Johnson was somewhat mollified, understanding that an occasional show of partisanship is needed to keep legislative troops in line.

He could work well on the telephone, too. When he wanted Frederic G. Donner, chairman of the General Motors board, to serve on the board of Comsat Corp., he at first got a no. Donner was too busy. A strike was threatened at GM, his board would never let Donner do it. "You spent sixteen billion dollars last year," said Johnson, brushing aside the protests. "You made two and a half billion dollars, and the only fellow in the country who operates a bigger business is talking to you right now on this telephone. This country allows you to do that, and it protects you, and I just can't have the most qualified man in the country tellin' me 'no.' I won't take it." The President called back in a few days, and that time he got the answer he sought.

Johnson sent his men into battle with the same kind of exhortation. Shortly after he had made Larry O'Brien Postmaster General, a drive developed on the Hill for District of Columbia home rule. Unable to move the measure out of committee, the White House backed a discharge petition in an effort to get the bill to the floor for a vote. O'Brien was still in charge of Johnson's legislative forces, and one day the President called him up. "You're a big shot now, Larry. Don't tell me you don't have more prestige up there since you've been Postmaster General than you did as just an employee down here. Let's get to work. Let's not let them get out of session until this thing is wrapped up." Johnson read off his list of prospective signers. "I don't want their signatures Monday, I want them now. . . . Frank

Thompson is in the hospital. Let's get him down there.
. . . Edith Green said see her after you get some others.
Let's see her."

Johnson used his devices on General William Westmoreland when he met with him in Hawaii in their first
intensive mutual confrontation. "I will give you everything you want, because you want what I want in Vietnam," Johnson told the General seated across from him.
"But I may have to give it to you a little slower than
you want." The President then sat back and fixed his
eyes on Westmoreland to see how he would respond.
"Mr. President," said Westmoreland, "I may not want
it as fast as you think I will. We cannot bring it in faster
than Vietnam can absorb it." Johnson liked that reply.
"That's the perfect answer that I need to tell the people
back home," he said. "I mean it," said Westmoreland.
A broad smile spread across Johnson's face and he
turned to McNamara. "You know, I ought to see more
of this fellow."

Applying the Johnson "treatment" to bring about his
coveted consensus was possible within the top rungs of
the government, even within the national leadership
community. But Johnson ran into trouble when he
tried to use his eyeball approach on the voters. He had
the notion that when he stood before great crowds and
used his familiar techniques with a little extra razzle-
dazzle, the thousands who looked up would get the same
electric charge that someone received inside the Oval
Office. There were moments when it seemed that it
might work as Johnson warmed up for his 1964 cam-

paign. His initial forays into the countryside—particularly a trip to New England in late summer—produced mass gatherings: folks apparently hungering for leadership, wanting to come out and somehow attach themselves to the person who had replaced John Kennedy, whom they now realized they would gravely miss. Those first encounters between Johnson and his audiences were wonders to behold. The President used his most dynamic stump style, telling stories, making promises. Instead of being won over, as those within the President's office often were, the people were at first stunned, then fascinated, then bored. As 1964 wore on, an obvious lethargy set in. He desperately tried to convince reporters of the national unity whenever he drew a large crowd. Jack Valenti supplied crowd estimates, hustled photographers and reporters to vantage points so they could see the throngs better and thus report Johnson success. LBJ called correspondents and cameramen into his car so they could sense the outflow of affection. None of it was convincing.

To Johnson, a crowd was to be breathed on, shouted at a bit, poked, amused, overwhelmed. That is why he raced from place to place, trying to encompass the entire nation. He was applying the "treatment" from Maine to California. He created huge contradictions in his quest to be all things to all people, such as preaching economy and more spending almost in the same breath. Despite the slow disintegration of his consensus and the apparent failure of his overheated salesmanship, Johnson could never break himself of the habit. His trip around the world in 1967 was an attempt on a global scale to win a little consensus. He wanted in that pre-Christmas rush to get everybody under his tent, to sweep them along with him in his great quest for peace and good will toward men. The result was much the same as in his domestic spectacles. He stood in Vietnam one day and praised his flyers and the effectiveness of the aerial war they waged against North Vietnam. A few hours later he was in the Vatican talking peace with Pope Paul VI, who the day before had asked for a bombing pause. To any thoughtful onlooker there was an aura of improbability about it.

Johnson's attempts to manipulate crowds were fascinating to watch. There were no individual people in the crowd for him; indeed, each assemblage became like a single person seated across his desk. The crowd had a personality, a position on each issue, a financial status and a distinct voice. Johnson tried to address himself to the personality. The hands outstretched to him, the voices raised slid off his consciousness as if it were glazed. Now and then a Texan or a child would arrest him for a fleeting moment and he would focus on one person. But most of the time the vast blob of people was the thing that had to be contended with.

Even in the unnatural state of consensus welded by Kennedy's death and by Goldwater there were evident strains. Johnson himself apparently sensed that trouble might develop. He constantly exhorted his staff to move fast, to get things done quickly. "We are not going to have this charter forever," he would say. "This will dissipate." But he worked frantically to hold the consensus. The intellectuals were his biggest problem from the start.

Consensus was not their way of life unless it occurred naturally, and that happened so rarely that it was suspect. Dissent to the intellectuals was nourishment. They resided in the world of thought, and that had no encumbrances. Johnson was charged with running the machine. He had to get things done and, as an immensely practical man, he resented any obstacle. He never understood the sheer exercise of dissent. He never had the time on his hurried way. "I'm the only President you've got," he told one guest. "Why do you want to destroy me?" Many of those who came to see him in his private moments urged him to look on dissent as a necessary part of national life, to listen and absorb what was good—if anything—and then go on the way of his choosing and not worry. But Johnson could not restrict his vision that way. He was driven to convince every doubter. At the urging of his aides, he spoke out on the right to dissent. But it was unconvincing because in the background he kept up his steady drumfire against those who disagreed with him. There was no small amount of inferiority complex involved. "I thought my speech in Baltimore [his appeal to negotiate the Vietnamese war anywhere at any time] would satisfy Lippmann," he said after the Johns Hopkins address. "I went over it with him, but I find out now about Mr. Lippmann and Martin Luther King and some others— old slow me just catches up with them, then they are

gone ahead of me." The Eastern intellectuals still bothered him. There was a story that he told frequently, and
at the end he always laughed loudly, too loudly—he
obviously was only half joking. He had gathered his top
men at the Cabinet table, he said, and there were
Rhodes Scholars, men from Harvard, Phi Beta Kappas,
and then there was one from Southwest Texas State
Teachers College.

He was serious one afternoon when he said very early
in his Presidency, "I'm not sure whether I can lead this
country and keep it together, with my background." He
paused during one of those soul-cleansings after the day's
work was done and looked far off and in a very subdued
voice said, "I do not think that I will ever get credit for
anything I do in foreign policy, no matter how successful, because I did not go to Harvard." There was truth
there—too much for comfort in this age. But there was
also tragedy. The Arthur Schlesingers and the John Ken-
neth Galbraiths displayed to him sometimes an almost
intolerable arrogance and blind conceit in their so-called
regional superiority. But that Johnson let it bother him,
that he did not appeal beyond them to a vast majority of
intellectuals who welcomed Johnson's Presidency, is
largely the fault of Johnson himself. He imagined more
disenchantment than was there. He suspected every man
with an advanced degree or some franchise from a campus. When two or three of those invited to the White
House Festival of the Arts sounded their sour notes on
Vietnam, Johnson was ready to condemn all four hundred of them and cancel the show. Eric Goldman, the

White House intellectual-in-residence, wisely talked him out of such a rash action, but LBJ then never forgave Goldman, counting him an equal traitor. Goldman almost by necessity assumed the role of martyr and eventually left the White House with a departing blast at the President's failure to comprehend the intellectuals and make space for them under his broad canvas. Historian Goldman found that Johnson wanted ideas only in the sense that they would tell him what to do tomorrow. He had a curious lack of interest in the intellectual process, the Professor felt. Nor did Johnson have a very acute sense of history, Goldman suspected. He found out, however, that Johnson would take notice of certain historical concepts if they could be related to other Presidents. If it could be pointed out how Woodrow Wilson had hurt himself when he tried a frontal attack on his Senate critics, then Johnson was impressed. If certain actions by Franklin Roosevelt could be related directly to his rating of greatness by historians, then the President took interest. But Goldman also observed that Johnson's established patterns of thinking, most of them rooted in the New Deal, tended to endure, reasserting themselves even after Johnson had publicly endorsed new ideas. The split widened with Vietnam and, indeed, with every irritation from then on—riots in the cities, the failure to raise taxes, rising prices, farm depression.

The press was lumped in with the intellectuals in Johnson's scorn. He defined the press roughly as the columnists. And when they failed to respond to his entreaties, as Walter Lippmann failed to in the wooing before the Johns Hopkins speech, the President was indignant. He felt the same anger when he entertained reporters at the ranch or the White House and then they went out and wrote harshly about him. In Johnson's world, where you made a deal—give something, get something—there was no excuse for such bad manners. "Why, I had that man at my table and then he went out and did that," he said one time over a critical news story. His idea of great flattery to a correspondent was to take the man under his arm, wine him and dine him and entertain him, treat him to a few innocuous secrets, and then suggest a story line. If it came out as Johnson wanted it to, he invited the fellow back for more intimate moments. And that time there was apt to be a call from the President himself to the publisher or editor of the man's paper and a spirited Johnson tribute over the phone. How little Johnson understood the responsible press was evident when, with the reporter listening, he passed out his most lavish praise. He would tell the publisher or editor that this correspondent was the best in the White House press corps because he had written that story just the way the President of the United States wanted it written. Any self-respecting editor, of course, made a mental note to consider shifting such a reporter from the White House beat. Any self-respecting reporter tried to avoid such suffocating embraces in the future. Unfortunately, too many editors and reporters liked to get those telephone calls and liked to hear that kind of tribute.

But Presidents can live without intellectuals. Franklin Roosevelt did, to some degree. So did Kennedy. The press, despite the abuses, is reasonably fair, and so even under Johnson's repeated provocations he was not harmed.

The business community was a far different story. The economic engine was needed for Johnson's success, and he understood that perfectly. He used all his cunning and all his persuasive powers to win and hold the businessmen. He was successful to an amazing degree. In fact, the most striking political phenomenon of his first years in the White House was the weld between factory and White House that this Democratic President was able to establish. One of the unforgettable scenes of the 1964 campaign was Lyndon B. Johnson in Detroit, standing before a roaring audience at the airport with Ford Motor's chairman, Henry Ford II, on one side holding up one hand, the United Auto Workers' Walter Reuther on the other side hoisting the other hand. Nobody was more astounded and gratified than Johnson. "Did you see that?" he asked. "I never had it so good." He was right.

For one thing, Johnson's own hunger for riches and his great success in getting them had left no room for hostility toward the business community. He had wanted to be a part of it from his beginnings in politics, and he knew that belligerency was hardly the way to the bank. He was thus solicitous, kindly, sympathetic, applying with marked emphasis the same soothing balm that he used in other areas of his political life. When he

89

was well on his way to big money he joined the ranks of the rich with gusto, buying land, cattle, airplanes, banks and other interests in a profitable maze of ventures that made him fully appreciative of the need for daring and for profit in the capitalistic world. He felt that his "ultimate" mentor, Franklin Roosevelt, was wrong in warring against the businessmen. Nor was Kennedy's attack on big steel in the spring of 1962 necessary, in Johnson's judgment. Johnson came along at a propitious time. Businessmen were a good deal more eager to listen to the government in his day than even under Kennedy. The upper reaches of industry were acquiring a majority of enlightened young men who understood the necessity for a link between their citadels and Washington, and the need for business to develop a social conscience. The wisdom of the new economics which Kennedy had preached in his famous Yale speech about old economic myths and for which he received some harsh criticism was obviously working, and nothing brings religion to a businessman quicker than profits. The Keynesian doctrine of public involvement in the economy had become not only acceptable but necessary. Johnson harvested all these benefits. Besides, his image as a multimillionaire entrepreneur had become quite well established and businessmen counted him one of their own.

On rare occasions Johnson articulated the evolution of his business attitude. It was a marvelous mixture of folklore, common country sense and the shrewd lessons learned in the committee rooms of Congress. The payoff was the splendid rapport of White House and board room. "The average businessman is kind of proud when he goes home that he can go in and see his little daughter at night, and not have people sayin' they are thieves and Al Capones," Johnson said. "They are proud that twenty-five hundred have been over here eatin' with me."

Johnson came to Washington with the Texas land baron Richard Kleberg, and it was his introduction to the world beyond Texas. "It was probably the first train ride that I ever took. It was a long trip for a country boy." As Kleberg's secretary, he was just down the hall from the House Banking and Currency Committee, which was then conducting hearings on the Holding Company Act. The young Lyndon Johnson was fascinated by the big businessmen, the grand names of industry and finance such as J. P. Morgan and Owen D. Young of General Electric, who came stiffly to the committee chambers. When he could, he took time off to listen. "They were all scared," Johnson once recalled. "They were scared of the government and everybody. . . . A businessman gets himself a little bit of money and he's afraid someone's going to take it away from him. He's worked all his life accumulating something and protecting it and hoarding it, and then his brother-in-law wants a job, and his chauffeur wants some of it."

As Johnson saw it, there was a predictable sequence. The businessman hired a bank to keep the money safe and next he found that he needed a lawyer to keep other people from taking it away. And the lawyer had to keep the businessman scared in order to keep his job. Then the businessman got worried about what the newspapers and the magazines were going to say about him. He hired a public-relations man to tell him how to handle the newspapers and the magazines, and the public-relations firm had to keep him scared in order to keep his business. He hired an accountant to tell him how to keep everything straight. Then he hired a Washington man so the government wouldn't take it away in taxes. Next he began to worry more and thought he ought to get one of the big firms, like Tom Dewey's, which really knew its stuff, and so that firm charged $4,000 a month and really had to keep the fellow scared in order to keep its commission. So every morning the man read a bunch of memos which gave information from "reliable sources" which weren't reliable but they all scared the hell out of the man and kept everybody on the payroll. So it went. The businessman was always looking around him—always wondering who was going to take that money away from him. But most of all the businessman was afraid of big government. Harry Hopkins went out and called businessmen names. Others said they were robber barons. Ickes talked about them and so did Aubrey Williams. The Senators picked it up and if the men weren't scared by then, they should have been. That four-letter word f-e-a-r was behind it all.

Johnson watched with some wonder. There were misunderstandings and unnecessary antagonisms. He never forgot.

"As soon as I came into this office," he said, "I decided the first thing I had to do was to stop businessmen from being afraid. After all, business makes the mare go." When Johnson summoned the businessmen in the tense days after Kennedy's death, he had a set little speech for each group. "We have a grave emergency. The President is dead. We have to work together to keep this country going. You have a big job to do and so does labor. I want you to make just as much profit as you reasonably can. If you make a hundred million instead of a hundred thousand, then Johnson gets fifty million instead of fifty thousand. There is no need to worry, because I'm not goin' to be goin' around tellin' you how to run your business. I think that you know better than I do how to do that and I believe that I know how to run the government, so let's leave it at that. You're not afraid of me and I'm not afraid of you."

Johnson hammered on his theory to the people in his government. He lectured to the regulatory agencies that their jobs were not concerned with going around the country making speeches that would unsettle businessmen. They were to make their decisions. If they had to take action against somebody, then go ahead and do it. "But there is no reason to go out and get them worried about what you're going to do or pass out any new philosophy, telling businessmen what they ought to be thinking and doing. Leave that to me. I'll give out the philosophy." He gave a similar message to the Justice Department's anti-trust division: do your work as you should, but don't go out so much talking about it. Johnson told both Secretary of Commerce John Connor and Secretary of the Treasury Henry Fowler to hold down public pronouncements that made businessmen nervous. "Let them alone and let them do their work," Johnson told others. "The businessmen have to succeed for us to stay free, for us to beat the communists. They've got to be free to compete, and they will beat the commies if their hands are not tied behind their backs. They are the best in the world at what they are doing. But they are the world's worst politicians and they don't have much social awareness sometimes—they don't give a damn for people. They are just interested in a little group of men over there digging a ditch or putting up a wall—how fast it is going, how much it is costing. But, hell, that is all right. That is their job. Politics and the social programs are my job. Leave that to me. I think those businessmen have come to believe that government does not intend to take their money. In fact they have come to see that they can have a bigger and bigger slice of an even bigger pie. . . . I'm not giving them a license to plunder . . . We just need to reason together."

Throughout his first term Johnson kept massaging the business community. There were on-the-record meetings and off-the-record meetings. The top business leaders made a steady parade through the Oval Office.

"Roger Blough used to come around ducking his head from side to side," LBJ once recalled, "he had been punched so many times. He doesn't do that any more. I told some of these pop-off artists to shut up. Now I get these businessmen in here every other week. So what happens? They finally come to discover that I know how to run government and they know how to run business and we trust each other. So when we have a welfare program going through here, I don't have Roger Blough and people like that down here telling me to oppose it. They let me run the government."

Once Johnson picked up a paper and read that the American Medical Association was going to boycott the Medicare program. He reacted in typical fashion. He called up the leaders and had them brought into the Cabinet Room, shucked his napping pajamas when he learned they had arrived, and hurried to talk. " 'Doctors are the most important people in the world. Why, doctors saved my life and they saved President Eisenhower's life. And I'm probably going to need 'em again. But doctors don't know anything about politics. Now, I just want to tell you what I will do. If you'll set up an advisory committee on regulations, I promise not to promulgate any regulations that aren't approved by that committee.' One old boy spoke up and said, 'I just want you to know how we feel about this.' And I said, 'I know how you feel about it, but you can't boycott this program.' He spoke up and said, 'I just want to tell you that we aren't gonna oppose you.' "

In his zestful style Johnson once explained why he put the government so forcefully into the negotiations between the steel companies and the unions. "Steel is grandma," he snorted. He had similar evaluations for other industries. "Railroads are grandma. Autos, aluminum, these other things, they are not grandma."

Johnson amused some businessmen, shocked others and even angered a good many, but, generally speaking, the business community realized that he was a friend. And speaking louder than any of LBJ's words were the soaring statistics of economic expansion, profits, personal income. When trouble began to pile upon Johnson, his strength in the business community was just about the last to begin to erode. Even in the dark months at the close of 1967 doubts had not distilled into bitter opposition, so strong was the link that Johnson had forged earlier.

REPORT

Lyndon Johnson had a singular love affair with the gross national product. He was called "the great consumer," because he was such an inveterate gadget man, reveling in all the labor-saving devices produced by United States technology. He had three-screen color television consoles which would beam him all three networks at once and with an automatic control he could tune in the sound of the one he wanted. Telephones popped out of coffee-table compartments, hung under his plates at dining tables, nestled in corners. He could talk on his office phone (which had thirty-seven buttons) without holding up the receiver. When guests wondered what POTUS meant, written out beside a red telephone button, they were told it stood for "President of the United States," a new internal code.

At his urging, the Signal Corps devised a monstrous speaker's stand which reporters nicknamed "Mother" because it enfolded him in sound-sensitive arms. Teleprompters rose silently from its top; an elevating device for short men folded out. No microphone was visible. "Mother" was tenderly wrapped in furniture padding so it could go with the President when he flew. Johnson

97

wrote with a felt-tipped pen, wore an alarm wristwatch, communicated on his ranch through short wave, enjoyed Muzak piped from the live-oak trees in the ranch yard, had six phone jacks around his heated swimming pool and a special raft for a floating phone. He drank from plastic glasses to keep his fingers warm, sometimes carried a transistor radio to get the news, tried contact lenses and had the cabin of Air Force One redesigned so it could be converted into a flying auditorium. The President had a special cold shower installed, a high-intensity reading light hooked up in his bedroom, special photographic floodlights recessed in his study. He carried an exercise bicycle on some of his long jet hops, adopted diet foods and low-cal soft drinks. And he proudly furnished state visitors with color photographs of themselves, made in the White House's own laboratory, only hours after they arrived at the front door of the White House. In California, after reviewing Vietnam-bound Marines, Johnson walked toward a helicopter and was stopped by an officer who pointed to another location and said, "That's your helicopter over there, sir." Johnson replied, "Son, they are all my helicopters."

ACHIEVEMENT

T HE GREAT SOCIETY was in Johnson's heart, but only vaguely in his mind. An accidental President. A great, raw man of immense girth wandering as a stranger in the Pepsi generation. Coarse, earthy—a brutal intrusion into the misty Kennedy renaissance that still clung to the land. Lyndon Johnson roamed the country in a green suit ("the Jolly Green Giant") in the age of muted gray. He was an avuncular figure who eschewed the seashore when the ads beckoned all America to seek the sand and surf. He had never skied in his life, and he hunted from the air-conditioned interior of a white Lincoln Continental. His golf was poor. Amid the great crush of culture, he knew neither Beatles nor Brahms. His artist was Norman Rockwell. He detested megalopolis and suburbia with equal passion. When media became the message, he still had a dust-bowl idiom. Quiet understatement and muted self-depreciation were the rage, so he had the Presidential seal emblazoned on cowboy boots, his rancher's jacket, cuff links, cigarette lighters and discardable plastic drinking cups. He proclaimed seriously one day that he was "the most popular Presidential candidate since Franklin Roosevelt."

Those who knew him had a certain admiration for this defiance. But not many knew him that well. Communication with his nation became a towering problem. In fact, long before the Vietnam war had stalled the Great Society financially, it had faltered in Johnson's own rhetoric. While he filled a fat legislative logbook and constructed through the use of his executive powers a commendable framework for his dream, he failed to implant it in the hearts of his countrymen. He could not talk the language or gain rapport with the age in which he came to power. It was one of Washington's fascinations to speculate on why Johnson, who had spent thirty-six years in the city and had learned better than any other man how to find his way through the corridors of power, had failed to adopt some of the sophistication and awareness that swirled about him in the capital. He had the intelligence for it. He also had the time. Yet he never would drop his hostility to this world. The more successful he became, the more defiance he showed. The more power he gained, the more he ignored the changing national customs. While he felt secure in his legislative world, he lost touch in an important way with the nation, and it happened long before he had a chance of being President. The result, as 1968 came, was that the impact of the Great Society was less than it should have been, even considering the Vietnam war.

His legislative achievement was shattering, and in the Johnson mind, still gripped by his Senate experience, little else mattered.

The $11.5-billion income-tax reduction measure was the lynch-pin of the new economics and provided the stimulus that sent the economy soaring to new records. Congress approved the Civil Rights Act of 1964 in the summer, a measure designed by Kennedy which covered public accommodations, hiring practices and voting rights. It was considered by some to be the strongest and most significant legislation of its kind in the century. Other important bills that were fundamental building blocks in the Great Society came tumbling from the Hill with astonishing ease, considering the stalemate that had developed between Kennedy and Congress. The Economic Opportunity Act of 1964, Johnson's poverty program, which also came from Kennedy blueprints, established ten coordinated programs designed to root out the causes of poverty.

There was a Mass Transit Act, a Water Research Act, a Wilderness Act. Johnson invited every single member of Congress to the White House at least twice in that year in an elaborate program of togetherness. When the year was over, *Congressional Quarterly,* a reliable scorekeeper of legislative activity, found that 57.6 percent of Johnson's legislative requests had been approved, the highest proportion of Presidential requests approved in ten years. That was nothing compared with what was to come.

Johnson's massive victory over Barry Goldwater

swept a great new majority into the House, a ready-made machine for Lyndon Johnson. His margin in the House was 295 to 140. In the Senate, LBJ had a 68-to-32 edge.

The President submitted twice as many bills in 1965 as he had in 1964 and 68.9 percent of them were passed, bringing the Johnson assessment that this was "the greatest outpouring of creative legislation in the history of this nation." Though 1966 was not as prolific a year as 1965, the White House claimed when the Eighty-ninth ended that the President had gotten 90 percent of the major requests. The legislation, indeed, had come like a freshet. There was Medicare, Federal aid to ele-mentary and secondary education, help for higher edu-cation, a farm bill, creation of new Departments of Housing and Urban Development and Transportation, another civil-rights measure—this one voting rights—Social Security increases, housing, an immigration bill abolishing old quotas, a program of aid for Appalachia, truth in packaging, demonstration cities, rent supple-ments, the clean-rivers measure.

Just about any record that could be conceived of had been broken by Johnson. In the fall of 1966 Larry O'Brien, the chief custodian of legislative matters, could single out the field of education. "No less than twenty-four major pieces of education legislation were enacted in the past three years alone. These laws not only removed from our political debate sterile argu-ments over church-state relationships, they also ended the old repetitive and largely empty rhetoric of States

Rights versus Federal Control. These laws, and others like them, signaled the birth of a new and more creative Federalism."

So much legislation was piled up that in the winter of 1966–67, while surveying his loss of four Senate seats and forty-seven House seats (plus his own precipitous slide from 80-percent approval to 44-percent), Johnson could honestly point out that the heart of the Great Society was passed. His legislative thrust in 1967 was toward consolidation, better administration and funding the programs that already had been passed. The four-year total, as tallied by the White House, was 226 major proposals passed out of 252 requests, for an astounding score of 92 percent.

But the Great Society as it stood when Johnson looked over his handiwork was not a total concept. It was a series of individual programs and ideas, most of which were commendable but which did not make a recognizable whole. Some of the promise of the Great Society could be detected, but the impact was hard to measure. Contained in the bills were the ingredients of the quality life which Johnson had sketched at Ann Arbor. There were attacks on the pollution of our environment, determined thrusts for equal rights and for better educational systems. There was a multitude of programs designed to relieve urban ills, and running through most of them was the realization that more initiative must come from state and local governments and that private capital must be induced to enter the arena. The old concept of the dole was all but abandoned in these schemes. Rent supplements—the idea of direct payments to families for housing, to vary as their earning power changed—was one of the most forward-looking plans devised in Washington in two decades. In Johnson's legislation there was emphasis on beauty and on culture. Men and women were encouraged to learn more, to improve their skills. There was the realization that more attention needed to be focused on children and youth to prevent odious problems later in their lives. The President subscribed, at least philosophically, to the plan to upgrade rural life so that migration to the urban areas would be retarded, thus preventing the inordinate growth of ghetto problems. Vice President Humphrey came up with the formula that $1 million spent in the countryside would save $20 million later in megalopolis. Johnson had endorsed the dignity of man and the pursuit of excellence. Yet something was missing.

There was no national sense of belonging to a new wave or of participating in a great social experiment. There was a minimum of excitement both in Washington and in the country. The great national energy was only partially roused. It was one of Johnson's bitterest disappointments. He wanted desperately to be a modern Franklin Roosevelt, focusing unrest and fragmented energies into a new crusade. He talked about building the Great Society on the foundations of the New Deal. He sometimes compared the Job Corps camps with the old CCC camps and the Neighborhood Youth Corps with the New Deal's National Youth Administration.

Vice President Hubert Humphrey one day sketched the kind of uplift which Roosevelt had brought and which Johnson longed to spark. He remembered that when he was a boy during the Depression in his father's pharmacy in Doland, South Dakota, he had sacked Paris-green insecticide (used to kill grasshoppers) until he inhaled so much he got sick. There were only hot sun and dust in his life then until a day when his father loaded him into the family Model A and took him to the edge of town, where the other residents were gathering in excitement. Men from Washington, sent there by Franklin Roosevelt, were going to plant the first trees in the great scheme for a fifty-mile-wide shelter belt that would run from Canada to the Gulf of Mexico and stop the billowing clouds of dust from smothering life on the prairies.

As Humphrey recalled, the trees died in a few weeks. The idea was a bad one. But that didn't matter, really. What mattered was that for the first time in years somebody seemed to care about the people of Doland, South Dakota, and that brought hope. The New Deal was in the hearts of men.

One of Johnson's obvious problems was that igniting people is a far harder task in time of great prosperity than in depression, when desperation dispels caution. The wealth of the United States and its effect on people were almost incalculable. Johnson got a taste when in 1966 he flew to Detroit for the traditional Labor Day rally. In times past, a President used to fill Cadillac Square with tens of thousands of cheering laborers. All that Johnson drew was a few thousand in Cobo Hall.

Later Walter Reuther explained that many of the men owned boats or lake cottages and certainly all of them had automobiles. Labor Day had become a real holiday for them. The last thing that Detroit auto workers wanted to do was come downtown to hear a political speech.

How much good could less than $10 million of Federal poverty money do in Cleveland, which had an annual area product of $6 billion? There was no viable calibration. But it was apparent that if, in the midst of such lusty production, poverty was still a problem (and it was) , $10 million was not going to solve it. The cost of rooting out the ills, the high price of administrative talent, consumed the Federal funds. Even if one could accept the highly padded Administration estimate that nearly $30 billion was spent annually either directly or indirectly (highway funds, Social Security payments and the like were included in this figure) in the war on poverty, it was a meaningless estimate unless one could get some notion of its impact on a nation with a gross national product that exceeded $800 billion a year. At least a few voices, like that of Senator Robert Kennedy, maintained that the ghetto problem was a $10-billion task by itself. There was a rather desperate feeling among some astute Administration officials that the true impact of all their programs was negligible, except in the obvious cases of Medicare and increased Social Security. While the vast majority of the population went about the task of getting wealthier, the ghettos were inflamed. Riots swept the country. The rehabilitation efforts in places such as Los Angeles' Watts area hardly seemed to make a difference. In the lush and sprawling suburbs where a third of the people lived by 1966, most of the families had no contact with the Federal programs against poverty and only very limited knowledge of what they were all about. The call of the Great Society in other matters such as pollution control and improving transportation was far off and appeared in headlines but not in daily life. On Thanksgiving weekend in 1966 one of the most monstrous traffic jams the East Coast had ever seen occurred. From the Baltimore bay tunnel thirty miles to Washington, D.C., cars were bumper to bumper. And about the same time New York was smothered in the most poisonous smog of its history. Crime on the streets went up, and the right of assembly was violated more and more by extremists. Lyndon Johnson, worrying about the activities of black-power advocate H. Rap Brown, put a shrewd finger on one aspect of the troubles. "I thought Rap Brown was a job for a local constable," said Johnson when the Negro leader was exhorting his audiences to violence in Maryland. "Now, all of the sudden I find that he's my responsibility." The problems, so vast and complex, could no longer be handled in Washington by bureaucrats who, by necessity, had to make and apply blanket rules. Johnson was trying to shove the country toward more localized involvement, but the response was slow. And possibly the main reason it was slow was his old communication syndrome.

When he should have educated the population, Johnson preached to them. When he should have galvanized them with his language, he bored them with endless statistics. Johnson had a box-score mentality that he had brought down from the Senate. The measure of the success of a Majority Leader was the number of bills he passed. What the bills meant, what happened to the programs embodied in the measures, was not a primary concern of the Majority Leader. But the most important task of the President is to take an idea from the printed legislative page and turn it into a functioning part of national life. This is leadership, that mysterious executive talent which is made up of many intangible factors. Yet when Johnson assessed his record, both in private and in public, it inevitably came out in numbers of bills passed and numbers of dollars spent. His evaluation of the splendid achievements of the Eighty-ninth Congress too often dealt not with the thrust of the legislation toward national betterment but with a grand total of 200 major measures submitted and 181 passed for a batting average of .905. In Nashville he told a crowd that his record in education legislation was unexcelled. Then he summed it up thus: "We've passed more bills, spent more money, reached more people, provided more comprehensive efforts in three years than in the rest of history." There was a lot of truth in that, yet it was only part of what was needed.

His view of the Kennedy record, because it lacked impressive statistics, was not very flattering. Kennedy had passed the Test Ban Treaty and he had formed the Peace Corps. That was about it, as Johnson saw things.

There were brilliant and important exceptions to this tunnel vision. Civil rights were in Johnson's heart as well as on his legislative list, and he talked about them with profound effectiveness. Before a joint session of Congress a few days after Kennedy's death he said, "We have talked long enough in this country about equal rights. . . . It is time now to write the next chapter—and to write it in the books of law." He did that, but he did not stop there. He took a moving message to the people whenever he had the chance, standing firm even before Southern audiences. He directed his scorn on the Ku Klux Klan. "My father fought them many long years ago in Texas and I have fought them all my life because I believe them to threaten the peace of every community where they exist. I shall continue to fight them because I know their loyalty is to a hooded society of bigots. . . ." In private Johnson was even more vehement, and he explained his own deep feeling: "The Ku Klux Klan was at its height when my father was in the Texas Legislature. . . . They'd elected a couple of senators and they had power and position around. They threatened him. Those campaigns used to get pretty hot. Men were called upon and told they'd be tarred and feathered, and a good many of them, friends of ours, were. I was only a fifteen-year-old boy in the middle of all of this and I was fearful that my Daddy would be taken out and tarred and feathered."

There was movement in the nation after four years. The amount and its meaning in the country were severely debated.

There were 5.8 million undergraduates attending college—an increase of 1.8 million in that time. Four million older Americans received hospital treatment through Medicare, and more than five million received physicians' services. The Federal statistics showed that people were rising above the poverty line 2.5 times faster than in the previous four years—more than 5.7 million lifted above the line in those four years. Two million children took part in Headstart. The educational gap between Negro and white narrowed some.

Yet the outlines of progress were very dim, if for no other reason than that the great national debates centered on Vietnam and violence in our national life, and it was very hard to assign credit for advances. While the White House quite rightly pointed with pride to the longest economic expansion in our entire history, this prosperity, a very vital force in all of Johnson's programs, was essentially the product of the free-enterprise system and the strong private sector of the economy. The guaranteed annual wage which Ford Motor Company granted its employees in the fall of 1967 probably was as intense a blow against Johnson's ancient enemies of poverty, ignorance and disease as any new program the government launched in the Detroit area in four years.

Again, because of the immense and continually expanding wealth of the nation, one is frustrated in calibrating the forces. The President's talented aide Joe Califano, a genial attorney who had been stolen from Robert McNamara's staff, pointed out that more and

more resources were going into the troubled areas. In
1960 Federal aid to the poor totaled $9.9 billion. In
1968 it was $30 billion. In 1960 the Federal govern-
ment spent $6.6 for health; four years later it was over
$22 billion. And in four years a million Americans were
trained for useful jobs through previously nonexistent
Federal programs. These statistics were quickly forgotten, however, when crime and violence continued their
upward spiral, an epidemic of riots swept the nation
and such responsible people as Pat Moynihan and Richard Nixon warned of terrorism and a possible race war.

There was a vague feeling that the troubles were
outracing solutions at an alarming rate, that the Federal government really had no gauge of how much help
was needed or even whether help from the central government was the answer. It was increasingly indicated
that the size and complexity of the problems made it
very difficult for the Federal government to either plan
properly or execute satisfactorily. New York's Governor
Nelson Rockefeller, far advanced in his thinking, simply pushed ahead on his own in the areas of transportation, pollution, housing, education and crime and let
the Federal government come along later. More experts
called for the total approach—a partnership of Federal,
state and local government with the business, labor and
intellectual communities of each sore spot. The Federal
role was to furnish know-how and some funds, but let
each community be responsible for direction and momentum.

Johnson sensed this. Others put it into words for him.

In his 1966 economic report to Congress the President said: "The tasks involve new and growing problems of an increasingly complex and interdependent economy and society. Only the Federal Government can assume these tasks. But the Federal Government by itself cannot create prosperity, reduce unemployment, avoid inflation, balance our external accounts, restore our cities, strengthen agriculture, eliminate poverty, or make people healthy. . . . Only through a creative and cooperative partnership of all private interests and all levels of government—a creative Federalism—can our economic and social objectives be attained."

That was, perhaps, the most encouraging domestic development in four years. Califano in 1967 cautioned that "too many Americans are ready to make the President the Mayor of every city, the Governor of every state, the head of every school district and the chairman of every corporate board. In the last few years, we have learned that the Federal Government—particularly if it is to reach the individual—can operate most effectively, and in many cases only, with the states and the cities, the foundations and the private charities, business and labor, and hosts of individuals at the grass roots of America." What Califano saw developing under Johnson was what he called public-interest partnerships in which the private sector and the government band together to solve a problem that may not be of direct concern to either but is a profound public interest. The President initiated a job-training program that took the risks out of setting up new businesses and training the hard-core unemployed in and near ghetto areas. Business provided the continuing jobs in the area. Benefits, hopefully, would accrue to everyone. Such public-interest partnerships, Califano ventured, "may be the key to create a climate of action and constructive change to better the quality of American life." Without using the Great Society slogan, he was saying the same thing and in a way confessing the frustrations of the Johnson Administration in trying to implant its visions amid general abundance. Turning to Calvin Coolidge's "The business of America is business," Califano said, "We are moving to the more hopeful dictum that 'the business of business is America.'" This was underlined even more in Johnson's 1968 State of the Union Address, which presented a program calling for more private involvement in public programs than ever before.

One of the reasons he was compelled to head in that direction was the number of adverse headlines he was gathering, particularly in the poverty program. Rooting out these deep ills proved far more difficult than the Federal planners had imagined. It was plain that Washington simply could not map the strategy for each ghetto. The Chrysler Corporation, after experimenting with training mechanics from poverty areas in partnership with the Federal government, became unhappy with the red tape and decided to take on the program by itself. The nation's first Job Corps center for women in St. Petersburg, Florida, found it cost $9,612 a year for each of the girls it trained, an exorbitant rate as judged by the General Accounting Office. The University of Minnesota's President O. Meredith Wilson, who chaired Johnson's National Advisory Council on the Education of Disadvantaged Children, sent in a withering report following observation of summer-school programs for 2,500,000 disadvantaged children costing some $250,000,000, or 24 percent of the entire year's appropriation for Title I of the Elementary and Secondary Education Act. And then a Labor Department report showed in 1967 that a pilot program designed to curb ghetto riots and help the jobless poor was in trouble. The problem was finding and reaching the people. Half the forty pilot projects were on the fringes of failure.

The term Great Society had virtually faded from Johnson's official vocabulary as he approached the summer of 1968. Johnson looked a visitor in the eye and confessed, "I've got a communications problem." How that problem came about is essential to the understanding of how the Great Society, a splendid infant, was orphaned.

For a long while the thoughtful men of Washington had rejected the careless journalistic assessment that Lyndon Johnson was a consummate politician. The more accurate appraisal suggested that he was superb in the close quarters of the Senate cloakroom (as long as there was a pliable President like Dwight Eisenhower around) but in national politics he was abysmal. He could make a deal with another man, but he could rarely inspire an audience. He proved this in 1960 in his clumsy effort to get the nomination. He relied on the fumbling efforts of his Senate cronies. When Tom Dodd promised him Connecticut or Clinton Anderson assured him New Mexico was sewed up, he erroneously assumed it was fact. His in-house operatives such as Bobby Baker, the ambitious young man who counted his Senate votes for him, were equally inept. They fed Johnson fraudulent tallies of the delegates because they (include John Connally, who later became Texas Governor) knew nothing of the hard-scrabble politics beyond the cozy quarters of the Capitol. In Los Angeles in 1960 Johnson was overwhelmed by Kennedy, who actually had won the nomination weeks before. The Johnson campaign for the Vice Presidency was no better. His schedules made no sense, his speech subjects were infrequently pertinent. The twenty-six-year-old Bill Moyers tried desperately to insert some order into the chaos and managed to a remarkable degree to carry the Johnson convoy through to a sensible conclusion. All of that, however, was lost on Johnson, who went into the 1964 Presidential campaign as haphazardly as ever. He had no idea, for instance, what political polls were for beyond flaunting them when they were good. And in 1964 the news was so good that LBJ's natural exuberance led him to create huge charts of his favorable ratings and stretch them across the White House East Room; then he would bring guests into this lovely statistical panorama, seize a classroom pointer and romp down the line, chortling over his 83's . . . 72's . . . 69's . . . 78's. His campaign dashes around the country were unplanned, as were his speeches, but it didn't matter because Goldwater was spreading fear. Johnson used the same format in 1966. And then, finally, it began to matter. Once again he roamed the country at his whim. He didn't bother to announce where he was going. His speech subjects did not fit his locations. He paid minimum attention to the local candidates he came to help—he was more interested in reviving his own lagging Gallup ratings. The off-year elections of 1966 were a disaster by anyone's standards. He lost forty-seven seats in the House and four Senate seats. At last it began to dawn not only on the President but on a great many of his exhausted patrons that there was something wrong. It was essentially communication.

From the start of his Presidency, Johnson's language rarely fitted his actions. Certainly his rhetoric did not fit the age. When he meticulously followed carefully prepared texts such as the Ann Arbor charter for the Great Society, his messages carried through. But on his own he was a rambling evangelist of thirty years ago. His oratory had the flamboyant personal style of the Texas county-fair political circuit, devoid of much meaning, but long and loud. He seemed sometimes to sense his problem of words. While he still had the services of Richard Goodwin, he paid him the highest compliment. "Dick Goodwin," he said, "he's wonderful, that boy. He can cry a little. He cries with me whenever I need to cry over something." He told Goodwin he was more important than all the others who worked for him. Once, when the President wanted Goodwin to go to the ranch with him on a few minutes' notice, LBJ personally

packed some of his own shirts, shaving gear and a tooth-
brush for Goodwin to be certain he would come along.

The problem was far deeper, however, than just
speechwriting. Another element was the merciless television exposure that had developed since 1960. The full
effects of TV on politics still have not been properly
assessed. But at least some things could be sensed in
Johnson's term. Rather than making it possible for
a President to build any image he pleased, as some
political experts at first feared, the persistent exposure
on TV clearly stripped away the make-believe. The real
man stood exposed as no one in history had ever been.
While Johnson could carefully regulate the cameras in
the White House, he could do nothing about those
which greeted him in every city in the country, and just
about wherever he went in Washington beyond the
Mansion gates there was a camera crew to record his
words and his actions.

Johnson was intensely chronicled by the writing press
because he was hyper-active. He once gave twenty-two
speeches in a single day. A rather normal week's White
House output of words, by mouth and on paper, was
more than twenty thousand. His private backgrounding
sessions for reporters rarely lasted less than an hour.
Three hours was not unusual. One Saturday meeting
with staff and reporters went for seven hours, with
Johnson talking most of the time. This was too much to
be digested either by the media which had to package it
and send it over the wires or by the people themselves,
who were smothered in Presidential declarations. John-

son frequently impeded understanding of important statements simply because he refused to pause, and in the great thickets of oratory and press releases which he created there was confusion. Richard Nixon in the fall of 1967 could look down from New York and observe that the President should limit himself to a few important problems at a time and do those well rather than drown in a sea of trivia.

Perhaps the concept of the Great Society was destined for partial eclipse because it was stated by another man, not the President. Even from the beginning there were those who suggested that Lyndon Johnson and Goodwin's rhetoric were not in harmony, that Goodwin thought and wrote as one of the New Frontier, a Kennedy man, and not as a product of the faded but real frontier. The Goodwin language was Eastern and Ivy League rather than Texas Prairie. The great reception of the Ann Arbor speech might have been in part due to the lingering hunger for more of Kennedy's eloquence. Lyndon Johnson, striding around the back lawn with reporters barking at his heels, was a bit shattering to the populace at first, and the soothing Goodwinian phrases brought a focus and sensible calm. It perhaps is easy to overemphasize the role of language in the Presidency. Indeed, it was fashionable for a while in the Kennedy era to scoff at eloquence. Men who had been around the Capitol for several decades would tell you that in the end the only thing which mattered was what actions a President took, not how he talked or looked. Good language was lumped with "style," a mildly contemptuous term for what middle-aged writers and politicians claimed was Kennedy's only virtuosity. This was an erroneous judgment. Perhaps in an earlier age Presidential speech was less vital, but in Johnson's time language had become an integral part of a President's business. What he said and how were elements of leadership. The clear and cogent statement of ideals and ideas is perhaps a President's greatest challenge and can be his greatest power. Teddy Roosevelt was ahead of his time by about fifty years when he summed up the Presidency as a "bloody pulpit."

The Johnson who immediately entered the American living rooms on the printed page or through electronics was a confusing figure, certainly not compatible with the Great Society he was trying to sell. That society was a challenge. Yet Johnson insisted, like FDR, on making promises. He painted grim pictures of despair whose dimensions often went far beyond the actual state of affairs in this wealthy nation. He often missed his mark, focusing on the rural shack dweller when the symbol of this age was the ghetto dweller. He described himself as the great benefactor who would ease burdens through unexplained economic wizardry that would spend more and save more at the same time. It was Lyndon Johnson's improbable world.

There are in Johnson's long career a couple of dozen speeches which are considered by political students to be "basic texts" on him. Even before he gave his Ann Arbor talk he had gone to Constitution Hall just behind the White House to address a meeting of the

United States Chamber of Commerce. He called for a great society in that talk, but it was lost in a stream of consciousness that portrayed the WPA from the Depression, OPA from World War II days, his dollar-a-day work on the Texas road gang, bankers who fleeced "widow women," the crash of 1929, the click of the boots of the Nazi storm-troopers from the 1930's. He raised the "ancient enemies of mankind"—disease, ignorance and poverty—so many times that one got the notion a large segment of the United States was blighted. He told of "fathers who have eleven children and have only twenty dollars on which to support them." He cast himself as the preserver of the Depression gospel of frugality: "Tell your friends that you have an independent, tax-paying, light-bill-saving President in the White House." In these unregulated litanies of the soul Johnson always brought himself in as the shimmering example of the old verities. "I have a little house where I was born, the son of a tenant farmer, a picture of which is hanging up in my bedroom, because every night when I go to bed and every morning when I wake up, I call it the 'opportunity house.' No one could look at that house and the way it looks, and not say that there is still opportunity in America." When he had finished this remarkable speech, he gloated to a reporter, "I really milked that one—I put a little sugar on it, too."

As the tempo of the 1964 campaign picked up, he turned to the "you-never-had-it-so-good" theme frequently and of course always offered the "it-will-even-

get-better" doctrine which had been devised by Roosevelt. Standing on the steps of the Los Angeles City Hall,
he shouted to the startled audience, "We are going to
educate our people. We are going to give them jobs, we
are going to provide Social Security, we are going to
give them more leisure time, we are going to improve
the countryside, we are going to have more recreational
areas, we are going to treat all Americans equally and
then there won't be a single one that will want communism." His thoughts reflected an unquenchable portion
of positivism. "I don't believe in harassing people; I
believe in encouraging them. I don't believe in hating
people; I believe in loving them. I am not filled with
fear; I am filled with faith. I am not going around
grouchy, always doubting that it will work." Social Security, one of the greatest of FDR's innovations, was
always handily used by Johnson, but the trouble was
that many of his listeners just did not understand what
it had meant to the despair-racked people of the 1930's.
"I don't know how much you have—you may have some
debts and you may have a husband at home, and you
may have some grandchildren—but the thing that is
really important to every person out there in that audience today is that Social Security card, because that is
going to permit you to live out the twilight of your
career in decency and dignity without going to the
poorhouse or without having to have your kids come
and take care of you. . . . I remember when we had the
minimum wage up. We had a minimum wage in 1938
for twenty-five cents an hour. My Daddy was on his

deathbed and he died that night, and I was sitting there listening to the radio with him when President Roosevelt went on the radio and appealed to us to come back to Congress so that widow women wouldn't have to work in pecan-shelling plants for seven cents an hour."

Within his giant jet as he pursued the voters across the country during that fall, Johnson was even more a political fundamentalist marching out of the past. When he was told that the Congress had passed his anti-poverty bill, he chortled to those around him, "I have everything I want." Happy days were indeed here again. "I've got the best family a fellow could ever have. Everything is perfect. We never have a cross word in our family. So what right have I got to bitch and gripe?" The world just kept getting better. "When I get up out of that car, you can just see them [the voters] light up and feel the warmth coming up at you." All the terms were reduced to their simplest. There were three national concerns, he told some astonished newsmen one night. "Everybody worries about war and peace. The men worry about heart attack and the women worry about cancer of the tit." The campaign actually became a kind of emotional orgy for Johnson, and the longer he went on, the more of a personal camp meeting it became. "Those Negroes go off the ground. They cling to my hands like I was Jesus Christ walking in their midst."

In the final days of the 1964 campaign, when the crowds began to thin and the country was obviously beginning to be bored by the spectacle, Johnson sensed trouble, and in Madison Square Garden just four days before the balloting he again spoke eloquently of his dream. "This nation, this people, this generation, has man's first opportunity to create the Great Society. It can be a society of success without squalor, beauty without barrenness, works of genius without the wretchedness of poverty. We can open the doors of learning, of fruitful labor and rewarding leisure, not just to the privileged few, but we can open them to everyone. These goals cannot be measured by the size of our bank balance. They can only be measured in the quality of the lives our people lead. Millions of Americans have achieved prosperity, and they have found prosperity alone is just not enough. They need a chance to seek knowledge and to touch beauty, to rejoice in achievement and in the closeness of family and community."

That, however, was just about the end of a focused concept, of a whole symbol—things that are vitally needed in communication. Promises persisted. Unrestrained exuberance replaced thoughtful analysis. "The real guts of my program is four things," he said one night in March 1965, "jobs, schools, health and voting rights. I've got the greatest job bills, I've got the greatest health bill, I've got the greatest education bill, I've got the greatest voting-rights bill. . . . We've got a hundred others. We won't get 'em all, but if I get that school bill, that health bill, that voting bill, those job bills, I'm ready to retire."

As the months ticked by and Johnson won even more of his program than he had imagined possible, his dialogue with America turned back to the "you-never-had-it-so-good" text. By that time there were more reasons than ever why such an approach did not appeal to the people. Johnson's audiences, for the most part, did not want to be lulled from reality. Half the people in the total population of 194 million in 1966 had gone through high school, and ten percent had graduated from college. They were not only fully capable of understanding most of the issues of the day, but they increasingly demanded to be told the facts, no matter how grim. Johnson abhorred bad news and felt that the people should not be given the full details about most problems until the government had had ample time to study them and establish its course of action. There was in the White House, despite persistent denials, a definite lack of faith in the ability of the nation to perceive wisdom and understand the world. Johnson was not alone in that. The entire capital, in a kind of reverse provincialism, fancied itself so hopelessly better informed that communication with the Dubuque milkman was considered impossible and a waste of time. The opposite was quite true. In addition to the increase in formal education, the population had become informed and aware, if not always educated, through television and publishing to a degree that has never been fully realized by most politicians. The speed and depth of analysis of major events is another modern phenomenon that has outrun its creators. The Middle East crisis, for example, was brought instantaneously into the living rooms in color. The press followed within hours with analysis, and within days there were books that neatly packaged the whole affair. Only now is some assessment being given to the effect of televising the war in Vietnam. Millions sit in comfort with their cocktails each night and observe the death and destruction of the day before on some battlefield ten thousand miles away. Mothers and fathers, in some rare instances, see their sons struck down. In such a world, candor becomes essential.

There was no better illustration of Johnson's problem than in the fall of 1966 when the great unrest in the country over the war, the state of the cities, the relations between the races and our role in the world began to reach significant heights. The President went into Ohio to campaign for Democratic members of the Congress. "Count your blessings," he shouted into the fall air. "No people ever had so much to be grateful for as we do." Just a few miles and a few hours distant Bobby Kennedy, in far more rapport with the national state of mind, declared that the Democrats should be "the party of dissatisfaction. I say this country can do better; it must do more." Kennedy's popularity responded accordingly, and for a few weeks he led Johnson in the Presidential preference polls.

In the summer of 1967, following the Glassboro summit meeting with Alexei Kosygin, when the entire nation was feeling good about that cordial encounter, Johnson plunged right back into the old mire with a speech before the Junior Chamber of Commerce, a speech that flaunted America's materialism. "We own almost a third of the world's railroad tracks. We own almost two thirds of the world's automobiles. . . . We own half the trucks in the world. We own almost half of all the radios in the world. We own a third of all the electricity that is produced in the world. We own a fourth of all of the steel. . . . I would like to see them enjoy the blessings that we enjoy. But don't you help them exchange places with us—because I don't want to be where they are."

In the fall of that year he showed his own contradictory nature in a talk with a friend. They were discussing Negroes. "I always say that if you give a man something for nothing, you injure him more than the state," said Johnson, reflecting the new concept of welfare. But then he lifted an idea from his New Deal grab-bag and destroyed the sense of pertinency with a picture of Depression nostrums. "I'm looking for a plan so that every Negro who wants a job can go down to the Fourteenth Street Bridge, and trucks will pick them up, and they'll work under good supervision and get a day's pay. We want that in every city. The mayors can work them in the parks, the governors can put them on the highways, building rest stops. The Federal government will put up seventy-five percent of the money, and the local communities twenty-five percent."

The chorus of disenchantment rose. One of the most perceptive criticisms came from the National Committee for an Effective Congress, which declared in December of 1967 that there was a depression of the national spirit and the reason was the lack of a national purpose.

"The new elements in the political cauldron are difficult to define or measure, because they are more psychological than tangible, involving people's morale more than their material comfort. . . . Traditional appeals to economic well-being and promises to remedy specific grievances do not invoke the cheers they once did."

Bob Kennedy was not the most objective judge of Johnson's stewardship, but even before he declared his candidacy he wrote of the trouble in people's hearts: "Our gross national product now soars over $800 billion a year. But that counts air pollution and cigarette advertising, and ambulances to clear our highways of carnage. It counts special locks for our doors, and jails for the people who break them. It includes the destruction of the redwoods, and armored cars for the police to fight riots in our cities. It counts Whitman's rifle and Speck's knife and television programs which glorify violence the better to sell toys to our children. Yet the gross national product does not allow for the health of our youth, the quality of their education or the joy of their play. It does not include the beauty of our poetry or the strength of our marriages, the intelligence of our public debate or the integrity of our public officials. It measures neither our wit nor our courage, neither our wisdom nor our learning, neither our compassion nor our devotion to country. It measures everything, in short, except that which makes life worthwhile; and it can tell us everything about America—except why we are proud to be Americans."

In January of 1968, standing before the Congress and

the nation, Johnson said in the 181st State of the Union Address that there was a "restlessness" in the nation, something he attributed to the forward movement of the country. But it was far more than that, and the events of the spring would show him.

EPISODE

ON A WEDNESDAY AFTERNOON about four o'clock in April of 1965 the Johns Hopkins University talk was ready for advance distribution at the White House. And as a strange little prelude, the President dispatched George Ball, McGeorge Bundy and Robert McNamara to the White House theater to give some capsule background for the television viewers. These short performances were to be put on film and shown after the speech was delivered that night. It was an odd device. Some of the correspondents dubbed these spots "the singing commercials."

Misty rain grounded the helicopters, and Johnson sped in an eleven-car motorcade over the Washington-Baltimore turnpike. Shriver Hall Auditorium at the university was filled with 1,100 students and faculty, most of them unsuspecting of the importance of the night's pronouncement. The big TV cameras were rooted in the middle of the seating. The hastily rigged klieg lights drowned the small hall in glare. The President's podium with the Presidential seal had been carted over from Washington earlier and was all set. What was called "Johnson's cheering section" preceded

129

him onto the stage. First Jack Valenti inspected the speaking facilities. Then Malcolm Kilduff surveyed the black-shrouded teleprompters with their transparent screens. The reading copy of the speech was fixed to the lectern.

Lynda Bird Johnson came onto the stage in beige and black. Lady Bird followed in yellow and black. Luci wore green and black. Muriel Humphrey had on light lavender. The Vice President was suited in dark blue.

Johnson entered with head down, shoulders hunched forward. He offered a rather subdued smile, and then a grave expression settled over his face and it remained there all night.

"The war is dirty and brutal and difficult," he said. "Some four hundred young men—born into an America bursting with opportunity and promise—have ended their lives on Vietnam's steaming soil. . . ."

He lowered his voice. He squinted into the lights. "And we do this to convince the leaders of North Vietnam—and all who seek to share their conquest—of a very simple fact: we will not be defeated."

But his message that night was for peace. And it came in quiet tones. "There may be many ways to this kind of peace: in discussion or negotiation with the governments concerned; in large groups or in small ones; in the reaffirmation of old agreements or their strengthening with new ones. We have stated this position over and over again fifty times and more to friend and foe alike. And we remain ready—with this purpose—for unconditional discussions." That was his offer. To talk any time, any place, without any conditions. It was a durable blueprint that Johnson followed through the next years. That and a billion-dollar development scheme for Southeast Asia were the Johns Hopkins doctrine.

It was a melancholy night. He meant what he said. "We often say how impressive power is. I do not find it impressive at all. The guns and bombs, the rockets and warships, are all symbols of human failure. They are necessary symbols. They protect what we cherish. But they are witness to human folly. A dam built across a great river is impressive. . . . I have seen the night illuminated, the kitchens warmed and the homes heated, where once the cheerless night and the ceaseless cold held sway. . . . Electrification of the countryside. Yes, that too is impressive. A rich harvest in a hungry land is impressive. The sight of healthy children in a classroom is impressive. . . . This generation of the world must choose: destroy or build, kill or aid, hate or understand."

MONUMENT

LYNDON JOHNSON is a monument builder. He insists that when he has finished his great efforts some edifice must stand as a tribute to him. The seven dams and reservoirs, one named Lake Lyndon B. Johnson, along the Lower Colorado River in Texas are the crowning achievement of his Congressional career. The legislative box-scores of his Senate days are the monuments erected then. There is special pride in having achieved the first civil-rights bill in forty years of Senate history. His Vice Presidency was frustrating because he constructed nothing and not even a medallion endures. His great work in the Presidency was to have been the Great Society, or even the "perfect society" which he once envisioned in a burst of euphoria, but the Vietnam war soon made that vision cloudy. It is no wonder that, in the midst of his anguish over the United States involvement in the Far East, he should seek some suitable memorial.

Late one night in Manila, where Johnson had flown in October 1966 on his remarkable crusade across the

Pacific, Bill Moyers, who perhaps understood and translated the man better than any other person who worked for him, paused after a crushing day of sweltering diplomacy at the seven-nation Asian summit and said, "This conference is part of the process of the President's of raising a monument to his Administration, that monument to be the recognition of the Pacific peoples."

Operating partly on his visceral instincts, led by the sheer weight of events, Johnson altered the entire thrust of United States foreign policy. The nation's concern, for the first time in history, focused on Asia. It brought great consternation to men like columnist Walter Lippmann, who found that part of the world alien and none of our business, who still found succor in the fact that our womb was Europe and who believed that our first loyalty was to the civilization which had spawned us. Johnson was no more enthusiastic at first. He simply had to fashion something out of his Presidency, which was destined to be shaped by the war in the steamy jungles of Southeast Asia.

His grand foray across 26,000 miles and into seven countries did more than anything else to assemble his policy and put into broad outline his concept, at first cautiously but later enthusiastically accepted by him, of his Presidency. He drew the blueprint for his Presidential monument in actions and words while on a vast international political campaign of seventeen days. It was his most ambitious Presidential undertaking in diplomacy and in many ways his most successful.

There was much that was natural about his eyes-on-the-East declaration. It was the only part of the globe beyond the boundaries of the United States to which he had any personal attachment. Over New Guinea on June 9, 1942, he was an observer on a limping and beleaguered B-26 Marauder which had been sent out from Seven-Mile Drome Airbase in New Guinea headed toward Lae, and his coolness under Japanese machine-gun fire from eight Zeros won him the Silver Star. He lived as a junior naval officer in Melbourne, Australia, and force-landed with the Swoose, a dilapidated B-17 that was ferrying him on his inspection mission for Franklin Roosevelt. Johnson's first major overseas assignment from John Kennedy was a fact-finding and goodwill swing through Asia, and it was then that LBJ sensed the troubles stockpiling in Vietnam and filed his report that warned about the future. And from the start of his Presidency, despite his initial intoxication with the thought of remaking U.S. society, his most persistent and encompassing problem was the war in Vietnam.

From that and from the vision of his own greatness which he could never relinquish came a concept that outdistanced the messy war, the Dominican uprising, the Panama riots, the crisis in NATO, relations with the Soviet Union and even the crisis of the Middle East which was yet to come. In that "long reach of history" which aide Jack Valenti liked to talk about, it may well be the most significant monument to the Johnson Administration.

He had formal words for what he was declaring. In Hawaii, poised on the outer lip of the United States, he asked: "How well have we understood the complex causes of conflict in the Pacific's time of troubles? . . . How well have we understood the impact of West upon East? . . . Only by answering these questions with candor can we build solid foundations for our future relations with Asia. Only then can we understand the depth of the desire in Asia for independence, for modernization and for dignity."

He had very personal words too. "There's where the people are," he said on his huge jet rocketing across the Pacific. "American interests are where the bodies are." He explained that for years people like Henry R. Luce had told him to look toward Asia, that two thirds of the world lived there, and that until there was peace and security in that endless area, there would be none for the United States. In Hawaii he explained his own late discovery of this obvious truth. His people had come from England. And those he had grown up with in the Fredericksburg area of Central Texas were from Germany. "Asia was almost alien," he said. "We looked away from the Pacific." His journey to the East, he told correspondents later, was to get America interested in the Pacific. "We tried to get Harry Hopkins to take a look at Asia in World War II, but he never seemed to show much interest."

At Honolulu's East-West Student Center he could sniff the future. "I am convinced," he declared, "that we have now reached a turning point in Asia's history, in Asian relations with the United States, in Asia's relations with the rest of the world."

For Johnson everything leads back home and to those experiences along the Pedernales and to the people of Blanco and Gillespie counties, the "hard-scrabble" country. This newest idea was yet another step in his late-blooming conscience on civil rights and the races. As a boy, he saw and understood the hardships of the Mexican-Americans with whom he lived and whom he taught in high school. When political necessity forced him to reconsider his hereditary attitude of repression toward the American Negro, the Negro experience became simply an expansion of his Mexican-American experience. The same happened to "the little brown men of Asia."

As usual, he was best at explaining himself when he was aboard Air Force One, dressed in his gaudy lounging robe, surrounded by awed reporters, the trackless miles of the Pacific reeling by seven miles below. "Asians are sensitive people. Why in hell isn't the unity of Asia important? Marcos [Philippine President] said, 'You're all the time talking about the unity of Europe, why never about the unity of Asia?' When they see this big blue plane flying in, they're going to realize we're interested in the unity of Asia. There have been indications of the United States looking at Asia differently because of little brown men out there, as if they are in a different league. Some folks turn toward Oxford—the little Georgetown cult, the intelligentsia. They pride themselves on humanitarianism, but they sure don't show much of it. Oh, they'll go with me on feeding India, but not the Asian Development Bank or an outside aggression. They soured on Korea pretty fast."

That bulky, impatient man could see it all unfold in the years ahead just as he had seen it in his Hill Country when the dams stopped the floods, brought water for irrigation, sent power to the poor farmers to relieve their endless drudgery. He could in his more lucid moments, sipping apple juice and thrusting his nose over a moisturizer to relieve his shredded voice, envision power lines down the Mekong Valley, lush and ordered fields of rice and new agricultural crops, sanitized villages secure and happy. Certainly it was oversimplified, and Johnson understood that. But, as he explained time and time again, he could not function without such a vision up there ahead somewhere. The gunslingers, he had once said, never did anything good for his Texas, despite their rather colorful legends. What made his country go, finally, was the strength of the quiet people who farmed the land, taught the children, ran the businesses. It was that way in Southeast Asia now. In the Johnson scenario, the Viet Cong were the gunslingers and the first job was for the vigilantes to clean them up, and then the quiet people could come in and bring the abundance of peace. He was particularly enthused about the development of the Asian Development Bank. "Texas," he told his enthralled listeners, "used to hate to go to New York to borrow money. It's the same with the Asians and the West."

The political situation there wasn't much different than it used to be in Blanco County before the New Deal came along, Johnson explained. "Political power held by the few and the rich within a nation is power that will not survive."

All along the route of his mission he intoned the same scripture, and the farther he went, the more enthused he got. His strategy was to come as an equal among equals. He had adopted Walt Rostow's doctrine of strength through regional development. "We're not going to be Number One or even Number Two," he told his staff. "We're going to be Number Seven. . . . I'm going to see, to listen and to learn." One of the amazing things about that odyssey was that he did practice remarkable restraint. The United States had tended, he told a group in his plane cabin, to leave the impression of the big powerful Uncle Sam calling all the shots out there. "The allies in Vietnam have been underplayed. The Rockefellers own the Chase Manhattan Bank, but that doesn't mean they meet over there and decide policy for everyone else." No, his trip, and particularly the Manila summit, might produce what amounted to a message to Hanoi that it must contend not only with "this dictator Johnson with the long nose back there in Washington" but with the others as well.

"Let us listen when the Asians speak for themselves," he said at the outset. "What do they want? They have told me. They want to be secure from outside attack. . . . They want their children to get a good education. . . . They want to be able to see a doctor when they are ill. . . . Disputes settled by other than peaceful means are disputes that will remain unsettled."

Halfway through his crusade he paused in Manila, and he had not changed his mind but strengthened it. "I remember Corregidor very well. It was the first time that the blood of white men and brown men was mingled in a common cause side by side. That is happening in Vietnam once again. I hope it is the last time. . . . But there is no reason because of the color of a man's skin for either doing this or not doing that. . . . Let's stop being defensive about our position. Every day I am instructed by *The New York Times* what else I should give up in Vietnam. I am tired of feeding the ego of *The New York Times*. Why don't they start asking what Hanoi is going to give up? . . . I'll do anything except swallow my honor and betray my country to get peace."

It was an Asian political campaign. Johnson was on the stump. His style was that of a country candidate, modulated a bit by his years in the Senate and the natural restrictions of being President. His caravan of five huge jets offered the natives the kind of spectacle that Johnson loved.

If eloquence was not always in abundance, or even if good taste sometimes faltered, it was nevertheless pure Johnson and it was drama of raw energy and a remarkable amount of sincerity. Because of that it succeeded.

It was a remarkable adventure also because it was the most coherent and logically sequential diplomatic effort of Johnson's Presidency. The trip was thoroughly thought out by the State Department and the ground was meticulously prepared in advance by Press Secretary Bill Moyers. The Manila summit, around which the whole thing was constructed, was planned with care. The event flowed from restrained start to reasonable end, giving a sense of purpose that sometimes was lost in the President's usual "herky, jerky diplomacy," as the Chicago *Daily News*'s Peter Lisagor once described his rambunctious travels.

He stepped into the Asian Pacific on American Samoa, where the natives came in their lava-lavas and sheltered themselves from the heat with banyan leaves. Old Rain Maker Mountain, which W. Somerset Maugham had made famous, looked across the bay at the colorful ceremony when Johnson went down a tapa-cloth carpet, touched the ceremonial cava bowl to his lips and greeted each of the hundred smiling tribal chiefs. This was a splendid and serene way to start a journey. Cars were festooned with flowers, the ocean was a vivid blue-green, all of the stuff of legend and romance was there. But it was not what Johnson was seeking, and that was evident on his face. He wanted the roaring adoration of great crowds. He sought motorcades through jammed streets and the homage of important people. This was the one major flaw—so soon apparent—that marred his Asian exploration. Somehow the spirit of adventure was not in him. The sheer joy of going to foreign lands and seeing what others look like, what they do and what they say, never moved LBJ. He went, as he did everything, to get something. He was, sadly, mainly interested in Lyndon Johnson and what it all meant for him. When he did not feel that he was getting a proper return on his investment, when he had only a handful of natives around him and there was nothing for him to do but inspect their simple homes or view their handicraft, Johnson's interest waned rapidly.

In New Zealand the President's eyes lighted up. Wellington, a kind of down-under San Francisco, exploded. He called for a CBS camera crew to jump into his limousine and view the surging well-wishers. The grunting photographers wrestled down to the floor of the car, straining their equipment to get pictures of LBJ and Lady Bird waving out at eager faces. "Ever see crowds like that before?" he asked the cameramen. There was a muffled "No, sir" from the floor. "You never will again," assured Johnson.

All the trappings of a United States political rally were in New Zealand, so Johnson joined in. When he met Norman Kirk, the Opposition Leader, he said, grinning, that he was a great friend of Everett Dirksen, America's sort-of opposition leader. "I don't know what Dirksen may be doing while I'm away," he said, winking. Then he took his forefinger and drew it across his throat. At the state dinner one bold lady—and they were mostly that way there—came to Johnson and said, "You're doing a helluva job." Sir Bernard Fergusson, Governor General, raised his glass to the glowing visitor. "The President is not tired," he shouted. "He is supernatural." The audience roared back, "Hear, hear!" This was what Johnson had come to find. There was a tongue in cheek now and then, but not often enough to notice. Barrie Watts, columnist for the *Dominion,* Wellington's morning paper, wrote, "He walks in a hippy, loose-shouldered way, winks and grins at starched dignitaries, lunges and chews, drawls, as he says, 'Good to see y', glad to be among y'.' All that's missing is the horse." But such flippancy was washed away in comments like the one offered to a newsman by an enthusiastic lady admirer: "He's the best hunk of flesh that's ever been in New Zealand."

New Zealand had been a preview for Australia. And despite a few ugly moments, like the red and green paint splattered on his car in Melbourne, Johnson found himself a true-to-life hero. "If I ever get kicked out of America, I'm coming to Australia," he said when he had finished his stay. He almost meant it.

In that raw, surging land Johnson dropped a good number of his inhibitions. He was a cowboy at a firemen's carnival. "Hurray for Australia!" he roared to the thousands and thousands of people lining the streets. "The Aussies were my brothers then and now. . . . A is for America, A is for Australia, long live AA!" As he went from city to city, the recall of his war exploits became more pronounced. That is a GI phenomenon, and the President of the United States can't be expected to be different. He told the audiences how he had arrived twenty years before in a sputtering PB2Y2 in rain and fog. "The Japs [he kept forgetting they were our friends now and were called Japanese] were just thirty miles away over the Owen Stanley Range in New Guinea," LBJ would say, letting a little breathlessness creep into his voice. He would then tell how the brave Aussies and the brave Americans threw them back. By the time he was ready to leave Australia, he was shoulder to shoulder in the trenches with the Aussies and

one needed only the barest imagination to envision
Lyndon Johnson standing singlehandedly between victory and defeat in the Pacific. While any President
would have been hauled mercilessly before the daily
journalistic court for such exaggeration in this country,
down there it seemed to fit the whole image of Big
Daddy from the United States. No one blanched.

In Canberra, Johnson talked seriously. "There is a
widening community of people who feel responsible for
what is happening in Vietnam. . . . The unilateral use
of power is out of date in an age where there can be no
losers in peace and no victors in war. And the unilateral
reach of compassion is limited. What is required—and
what we are seeing emerging in Vietnam and throughout all of Asia—is a concert of effort on the part of
diverse nations that know they must work together."

In Melbourne some enthusiast produced fifty-seven
beagles in tribute. "He's a good bloke," said a woman.
And Prime Minister Harold Holt, grinning, puffing to
keep up, slightly appalled but more fascinated than
anything else, confided to his Parliamentary friends,
"He's the biggest fish I ever speared." If Johnson heard
that, he probably appreciated it as a politician's compliment. Angry dissenters nearly marred his visit to Syd-
ney, but alert police and good drivers avoided real
trouble. Most of the town enjoyed the visit, and the dignitaries gave him two kangaroos. When he was asked
what he would do with the animals, he roared, "Hell,
I'll put them on the ranch and I may ride one of them
down to the Post Office at Hye."

Johnson may have jarred the natives a bit when he showed up at a barbecue in his rancher's twill, Texas hat and boots and a huge, glistening Presidential seal embroidered on his jacket over his heart. Still, even in that kind of lawn-party atmosphere there was a sense of awe and admiration for the big American who was standing hard in Vietnam. If Johnson's native arrogance offended Holt, the Prime Minister never showed it, and there was occasion. Flying on Air Force One with the Holts, LBJ was heard to say, "I like to come out and look my Prime Ministers over." Nor did Mrs. Holt flinch when, after explaining to a reporter how much she liked American bacon, Johnson reached over and speared one of her slices as she breakfasted on his plane. Finding the bacon very tasty, the President ordered another helping for himself, but no more for Mrs. Holt.

Manila was to be the capstone of the great Pacific mission. There vigorous regionalism was to be asserted, firmness against aggression to be restated, a grand charter to be drawn pointing the way for more development in the Pacific. To a degree, all of this was accomplished. Manila was a successful meeting, and much was due to the restraint that Johnson imposed upon himself. "He's a twenty-percent man on this trip," said Moyers. "He's going to listen eighty percent, talk twenty percent." He may not have talked that much. One Filipino writer, after almost two days of meetings, reported on Johnson's behavior: "Mr. Johnson has been heard to cough slightly, but presumably this is not expected to dictate the course of the conference." LBJ was determined not to dictate the terms or even appear to influence the course of the summit. Of course that was impossible in fact, since U.S. dollars and might shored up all those nations. Yet the United States' modest behavior was crucial to success. LBJ took the same accommodations as the other state heads, his only luxury being an over-size bed. He went to call on some of the other heads of state in the traditional protocol rituals, and he told them of his own shortsightedness for twenty years. He had, he said to South Korea's President Chung Hee Park, been blinded by Europe. For instance, he had op-posed admission of Hawaii as a state for twenty years. Since he had entered public life to help people, he went on, he had decided "the place to do it is in Asia. There's where most of the people are." Johnson maneuvered his massive frame so that photographs would not show him towering over the smaller Asians. He avoided, when he could, pictures standing shoulder to shoulder. He stood on the lower steps, looking up to those above him. He joined in the festivities, wore a flower garland, rode in a horse-drawn cart and sported the native barong tagalog. He thumped his points when he had a spare minute. "We can't lead them. We can't speak for Asia. All we can do is help them. . . . If we don't get anything else, the fact seven nations sat down together is something. . . . Developing regional pride is what this is all about. . . . It's like Baltimore got from winning the World Series."

What Lyndon Johnson saw in that meeting—indeed,

what he saw for all of Asia—he put down in his final statement before the heads of government. He had seen the emergence of certain principles in these talks, he said. He listed them. Resistance to aggression. Reconstruction and commitment to the job of pacification and development. Regional development. Reconciliation with the aggressors. "I have seen the banners that say 'We want peace' and I say, 'So do I,' " Johnson told the men seated around the meeting table. "I have seen their banners that say 'We hate war' and I say, 'So do I.' " Johnson had been given new foreign-aid figures to show how much we were pumping into the Asian economy, but these he discarded in fear that once again we would appear to be buying support. The United States of course was the major behind-the-scenes coordinator and drafter of the three-part statement that emerged from the conference. The State Department's Bill Bundy and the White House's Walt Rostow worked through one night. However, the leaders themselves did a surprising amount of editing in the next day's session, finding the draft too wordy and obscure in some areas, insisting on simplicity and in the end deciding on a "Goals of Freedom" statement that began: "We, the seven nations gathered in Manila, declare our unity, our resolve, and our purpose in seeking together the goals of freedom in Vietnam and in the Asian and Pacific areas. . . ."

The most intriguing and controversial part of the communiqué came in Paragraph 29, which spelled out an offer by the allies to withdraw their forces from

Vietnam in six months if aggression from the north ceased and there was assurance, with the necessary safeguards, that it would not resume. Johnson had asked for that provision in the declaration. Before he came to Manila he had met with the Soviet Union's Foreign Minister, Andrei Gromyko, and Gromyko, after hearing the President's desires to leave Vietnam in peace, had told him, "You've got to be more precise, to spell it out." Johnson had decided that Manila was a good place to do that. The State Department was reluctant, wanting language to hedge. Johnson struck it down. He wanted it straight. "We're going to say, 'We will withdraw in six months,'" LBJ insisted. The South Vietnamese and the Koreans, the most aggressive of those at the Manila summit, were wary of Johnson's plan. It might be, they insisted, misread as a United States excuse to get out. "Nobody can accuse us of a soft attitude," said Johnson. "If anyone doubts the basis of our commitment, they will find that we have more troops in Vietnam than there are words in the new Webster's Dictionary." The six-month withdrawal proposal remained.

The lengthy statement was finally issued, but only after one of those comic operas that occasionally occur at such cosmic meetings. The mechanics of editing, duplicating and distribution simply broke down. There was deep suspicion that this was a deliberate ploy by the Filipinos to make certain that their news media got the word first. In any event, Bill Moyers typed the stencils and helped operate the mimeograph machines so that

147

nearly a thousand raging correspondents could write their stories.

In the midst of the Manila summit came the greatest act of the whole Asian drama. Johnson flew to Vietnam. The idea that he might visit the American troops there had been discussed before he left the United States, and most correspondents expected that he would find time on his way either from Manila to Thailand or from Thailand to Korea. There were, naturally, frightful security problems to such a visit, and there was less talk about it as the Johnson Asian tour arrived in Manila. The President himself had been ambiguous. He told friends that security was the trouble any way you looked at it. If he went, then some would say he was grandstanding, taking unnecessary risks. But if he didn't go, another faction would say he was a coward. The proper display of courage bothered Johnson, as it had John Kennedy before him and probably every President.

The hole in Johnson's otherwise frantic schedule was on Thursday of the summit week. Nothing was scheduled on that day but a leisurely trip to Bangkok. Tuesday night, as he was leaving the Malacañan Palace, the site of the meetings, he summoned Ambassador Henry Cabot Lodge, Dean Rusk, Bill Moyers and General William Westmoreland into the small office that had been assigned to him, and they talked over whether the President should make the flight. There was near unanimous opinion that he should, and Westmoreland spoke up for a surprise visit the next day. Johnson agreed, and

148

the secret mission was set in motion. Correspondents
were locked away from the public Wednesday morning,
whisked to Sangley Point Field on the far side of Manila Bay, there secreted aboard a Pan Am plane which
flew to Cam Ranh Bay to wait for Johnson. The only
clue the unsuspecting press had that morning was Johnson's haberdashery. He wore brown shoes with a dark
gray suit. It was so out of character that Peter Lisagor
commented upon it as Johnson went on a ceremonial
visit to Corregidor. But not until he was aboard Air
Force One jetting toward Vietnam did Lisagor learn
the reason for the lapse in style. The President emerged
from his cabin in his brown rancher's outfit, shoes to
match. Fighters screamed above the Presidential plane,
the Navy watched below. Without incident or advance
publicity, Johnson stood before several thousand of the
fighting men on the hot gray sand of Cam Ranh Bay.
Some of the GI's had been taken from foxholes that
very morning and rushed to the assembly area. Johnson
pinned medals on a few men, surprised General Westmoreland with a Distinguished Service Medal. He rode
beside Westmoreland in the back of a jeep, standing up,
gazing out over the strange landscape. In this moment
he seemed more inspired than anyone could remember
him being before. When he stood up before the men, he
visibly tried to suck in his sizable stomach and square
his shoulders to be a fitting companion for Westmoreland, who looked like a recruiting ad. "We believe in
you. We know you are going to get the job done. And
soon, when peace can come to the world, we will receive

you back in your homeland with open arms, with great pride, and with great thanks," Johnson told the troops. He rode slowly through the dying day, visiting hospitals, clutching hands ("How about one for Texas?" called out a GI, sticking his hand above the crowd). The smothering heat made Johnson sweat through his shirt. "Better tell him to take a sweat pill tonight," said a corpsman to a White House aide. Johnson joined the mess-hall line and ate with the men, who came with their M14's and M16's over their backs and slung the guns on their chairs next to Johnson. "I don't believe they feed you this well all the time," he said, and that reminded him of a Texas story. "One Sunday the preacher came to dinner at my house and my older brother said, 'I wish you'd come to dinner every Sunday because Mama doesn't feed us this well every Sunday.'" He was wringing wet by then, and in the purple dusk the jeep caravan turned on its lights. In the officers' club with the overhead revolving fans Johnson faced his field commanders—names like Walt, Larson, Seamons, Momyer. It was noisy, so Johnson had to raise his voice. "I thank you, I salute you, may the good Lord look over you and keep you until you come home with the coonskin on the wall."

In the dark, as Johnson's jeep drove slowly to his jet, the troop lines on the sides of the metal landing ramps cheered. Nothing had stirred Lyndon Johnson quite this much. His jet plunged unharmed back through the night toward Manila.

Unfortunately, the intoxication of such moments

fades fast with Johnson. He comes too rapidly back to self-contemplation. Even on the plane returning to Manila he told the correspondents that General Westmoreland had said, "This is the greatest day since I took command." The inference was, of course, that Johnson had done more for the troops than they did for him, which may have been the case, but was not one of the things that a person suggests. In the report to the nation which Johnson put on tape, he was even more carried away with his mission. He mentioned himself eleven times in the first few minutes and he gasped something like "Do you know that some of those men had just climbed out of their foxholes to be with me, they had just come from battle carrying their guns on their backs?" The White House staff mercifully cut that from the released version.

In Bangkok, Johnson lived in the grand palace complex, the setting for *Anna and the King of Siam*. A Secret Service man was overheard discussing the tradition of servants serving on their knees, and he chuckled, "This is Johnson's kind of place." LBJ watched the delicate Thai dancers and he signed the International Education Act on the spot, bringing a little United States political culture to the scene. The Thai officialdom had the same questions that others had had. Was the U.S. resolve unwavering? "My answer," he told them in private, "is three hundred thousand troops in Vietnam."

In Malaysia he helicoptered into the jungle which only a few years before had been overrun with guerrillas and had been untended. Now it was settled, rubber was in production. But Johnson was tired and the oppressive heat was too much for him. Clutching a battery-powered hand fan which he held in front of his long nose seeking some relief, he moved slowly and without visible inspiration through the tiny homes of Labua Jaya. He wore a banju shirt, sipped coconut milk, but besides his great fatigue there was the old fact that he couldn't get deeply interested. "Well, Judge," he finally said to his aide Marvin Watson, "is this all I have to do?" Assured that it was, he hurried away.

Weariness soon vanished in Seoul, Korea, when he stood at City Hall and viewed a huge reservoir of people, part of the reception estimated at two million. When Johnson asked for his favorite statistic, the size of the crowd, President Park and his officers apparently misunderstood part of the question. There was a hurried consultation and the answer came back that two million was all the people that Park had. LBJ thought that was a delightful joke and still tells it with relish. Everything pleased him in Korea, even the signs held by the schoolchildren: "Golly Cowboy . . . Texas Bull We Like."

On a hill hastily named "Lyndon B. Johnson" he gave a village elder an RCA table-model TV and, true to style, envisioned the time when power grids would cover the valley. He remembered Texas. "We were short of water, we were short of money, and many, many times we were short of hope. . . . What we did in my country in the '30's you are doing better in your country in the '60's." He gave the old man a ride in his helicopter. "Like going to heaven," Si Jong Chol said on the ground, gathering his robes about him and clutching his stovepipe hat in the gale from the rotors. Johnson gave the troops who guard the 37th Parallel a bronze bust of himself. He told them the Texas story of the quarterback "Hard Head," who reluctantly battered the line. He patted his own bronze pate as sculpted by Jimi Lu Mason (Air Force One came home burdened with busts, small, medium and large) and implied that he was their own "Hard Head," carrying the ball reluctantly, but carrying it just the same.

Johnson's enthusiasm in being with the men on the front lines overwhelmed him again. It was here that, recalling the military heroes of past days, he said his great-great grandfather had died at the Alamo, the fiction that later he would confess but not before all the American reading public got a good laugh. The misstatement would stick with Johnson, being frequently pointed out as one of the minor causes of the credibility gap. And, indeed, it was. The President wanted so intensely to be a part of the experience of the men and people he was talking to that he made things come out the way he wanted them to come out, not necessarily the way they were. In Australia he was in the trenches. In Korea his forebears were spilling blood at the Alamo. In Anchorage, Alaska, in telling a forgotten chapter in his history—of flying there with Senator Warren Magnuson just after the Japanese had taken Dutch Harbor in the Aleutians—Johnson drew an exaggerated picture of a mission into the darkest danger.

Yet in the blur and scope of a swift and grand mission such as Johnson had undertaken, such things are swept aside. The worst thing about his odyssey was his failure to establish a bond with some of the people and to react warmly to some of the things he saw. My old notebook has a passage, written at the time of observation. "One of those minor tragedies in the make-up of Lyndon B. Johnson is apparent on this junket. He just does not become engaged with the people he meets. He does not respond to their overtures, does not pick up opportunities to endear himself. It is obvious when you travel with LBJ that he lacks a certain sense of history and he also lacks deep interest in those he visits. His mind in on Johnson, not Pago Pago. His interest is personal, not in the culture. Johnson is too determined that he is going to prove that he is loved. Because of this itensity he sometimes misses the very best chances for things he wants most."

By the time Johnson's plane touched down in Anchorage he had labeled his trip "a momentous journey," and this was closer to the truth than some other of his sweeping evaluations. He had paid honor to all the countries that he had visited, had reaffirmed our determination, had preached a new interest in their affairs and had not come as a master to the slaves. Johnson had genuinely encouraged their own burgeoning self-pride and nationalism. The spectacle of a strong man had left its mark too. Few would forget the Malaysian mother who counseled her child, "You watch. You are about to see the most powerful man in the world. You will never forget this moment."

But more important than all of that was the defini-tion that Johnson gave to his foreign policy. Forced to live with it, see it, think about it and eventually talk about it without any domestic political diversions, he presented in the collection of his remarks, both in public and in private, the most complete picture yet of what he was reaching for—a dominant national con-cern for the Pacific and its people.

INCIDENT

WHEN RICHARD GOODWIN came back to the White House to write speeches for the President, I immediately went to his office to renew our friendship. I chatted beside his typewriter for a few minutes that he took off from writing a speech for Johnson which was to be delivered at the University of Michigan's commencement exercises. In private Goodwin was most candid about his duties, but the White House had not officially acknowledged his writing assignment, so to avoid embarrassing him I went along with the fiction and did not report Goodwin's actual work.

But the speech Goodwin had been working on when I talked with him was Johnson's notable Great Society speech, and such interest in the concept built up that I felt the time had come to examine publicly Goodwin's role in policy-making. I went to work on a story about the resurrection of Goodwin and routinely asked to see George Reedy, Press Secretary. When my appointment hour arrived, Reedy whisked me straight into the Oval Office for a face-to-face encounter with Johnson. LBJ's interest in what was written about his staff obviously was more than routine. There then followed a curious

156

ritual in which Johnson denied that Goodwin wrote
speeches for him. I said that perhaps we misunderstood
each other. Certainly a President's speeches were a product of his own thought and effort. But there was always
a writer somewhere who helped put things together and
polished the lines. For the moment Johnson's refusal
to admit the obvious was amusing and even understand-
able. But the President persisted. No, he said, Goodwin
didn't write his speeches. He was there for special research. Oh, yes, he might actually write a memo which
would be used in the preparation of a speech, but he
wouldn't write one. "To the best of my knowledge,"
said the President, "Goodwin has not written a single
speech for me. As far as I know, he had nothing to do
with the Ann Arbor speech." I was somewhat at a loss
for words. I looked rather blank. Johnson sensed my confusion. He turned to George Reedy and asked, "Isn't
that so, George?" Reedy made a sound which was neither
yes nor no and shook his head, neither up nor down, in
a way which somehow was an endorsement of what Johnson had just said without being an endorsement.

For a few minutes, as Johnson continued to talk
about his staff, I had the notion that he was playing a
game. He certainly knew that I was aware that Goodwin wrote his speeches and, indeed, had become his
chief writer. There is always a compulsion to sympa-
thize with the President, any President. In his presence,
particularly, there is a great urge deep down to believe
him. The atmosphere is so compelling. My immediate
conclusion was that he had some profound and impor-

tant reason to deny the obvious. Johnson wound up the interview by pulling a felt-tipped pen from his shirt pocket and sketching the table of organization of his men. Down at the bottom under a "Miscellaneous" category was a man named "Goodman." This was the ultimate put-down—misspelling Goodwin's name, as if he were a stranger in the White House.

CREDIBILITY

I T IS A SINGULAR EXPERIENCE to be told by the President of the United States—the most powerful man in the world—that something you know to be true is not so. Yet that is what happened repeatedly when Johnson first entered the White House. It is the essence of the credibility gap. It occurs still with alarming frequency and is why Johnson just cannot escape from beneath that dark cloud of unbelievability. The press, of course, was the first group to become aware of this habit of the President's. As the public's paid observers on the spot, they had an immediate dilemma in paying due respect to the Presidency and at the same time sorting out the reality. It was much like a drop of oil in tissue paper. Centered in the White House and Washington at first, disbelief in what the President said spread until it soiled the entire fabric.

My reaction to the Goodwin episode at first was to shrug it off as another of the hazards of covering that unusual man. It was a small fact to be included in the total equation. For some reason quite unclear at the time but perhaps explainable later in the context of the Presidency, I told myself, Johnson wanted to obscure certain of his activities and to do it he chose to mislead his questioners. One incident was not enough on which to base a judgment. But, unfortunately, that incident was only one among many. The steady procession of reporters and commentators through the Johnson journalistic salon of those days was bombarded with similar fiction—none of it very important. Almost immediately, however, a warning flag went up: the President's word was suspect.

Reporters were baffled from the start as to why the President did not simply refuse to talk about things which he felt should not be in public domain rather than stage elaborate dramas to present false impressions which inevitably were found out. Even a direct request to a reporter not to print something would have been accepted with more understanding than the sleight-of-hand which Johnson tried to practice.

Those who thought beyond the simple surface phenomenon developed various theories as to why Johnson would risk the reliability of his Administration in such inconsequential matters. The theories were many and involved. It became apparent early that Johnson was not one of those people who become so mesmerized by their own dreams that they actually believe their verbal concoctions. Just a few weeks after the Goodwin incident took place the President was bragging to other newsmen that "Goodwin can write a better speech than Sorensen and in one fifth the time." He had suddenly become proud of his possession and talked freely and accurately about Goodwin's role, spelling and pronouncing his name correctly.

Basic to the matter was Johnson's very simple belief that the ends justified the means. There had always been a question as to whether Johnson was more ambitious for himself or for his country, but that really did not matter, because he believed his greatness could be gained only by doing right for the country. His ambitions and his goals, in short, were noble. He very clearly understood and understands that if this country rises to greatness, he does too. The problem developed in getting there. In his limitless churning to arrive, he used almost everything and almost everybody in ways that frequently defiled his very dreams. There was great truth in the observation by one of his close friends that "ninety percent of what he wants is right but ninety percent of the way he does it is wrong." Those few true believers who still cluster around Johnson find their faith in that explanation. Somehow, after years of exposure to the man and years of troubled thought about him, they can appraise him with split vision, ignoring the methods and clinging to the hope of real and lasting achievement. Such an appraisal takes patience and long, deep thought—even prayer, as one Johnson partisan suggested. In my judgment, only a handful of men in Washington fully understand those dimensions in Johnson. That understanding has taken thirty years on the capital scene. The nation has known Johnson for only seven years, and the public is a lot less informed than the men who walk the back corridors of power.

The term "credibility gap," so devastatingly graphic, is one of those journalistic tools whose origins are shadowy. The Washington *Post*'s Diplomatic Correspondent, Murrey Marder, remembers employing it in December of 1965. *The New York Times*'s Reston used it in January of 1966. No doubt other writers put it in copy, totally unaware that their colleagues had arrived at the same designation. It is one of those natural phrases that come from the current idiom and the newspaper mentality. The term became a national symbol when House Republican Leader Gerald Ford employed it in one of his bare-fisted attacks on the Administration early in 1966. It was a crystallization of what everyone had sensed in the political world. The public was just beginning to grow uneasy.

In a curious way, the credibility problem arises out of the President's very faith in what he reads and hears— the media he vehemently blames for his troubles. A White House aide put it rather well when he told the Baltimore *Sun*'s Philip Potter: "Fundamentally [Johnson] believes what he reads in the papers . . . and he thinks the way to change things is to change what is printed in the papers . . . you can't trust people with the facts, but you can create facts that people will believe." This is a familiar strain, noted in the Boyhood Home. Things are to be represented as Johnson wants them to be, not as they are, and by the time his small hoaxes are discovered he has accomplished his purpose, the theory goes, and nobody will really care about his methods. That, as it turned out in the White House, is a tinsel theory.

No little bit of Johnson's difficulty with the facts is rooted in the frontier. Texas historian Walter Prescott Webb, in explaining the origin of the Western legend, emphasized that the people of the vast reaches of the Southwest had so little in worldly terms that they exaggerated whatever came into their hard lives. These frontier people were cozened by politicians, Webb says, frozen by blizzards, eaten out by grasshoppers, and about the only way they sustained life was in their imaginations. Bootleggers, gunmen, drifters and grafters became men of legend, blown up like photographic enlargements far beyond the original dimensions.

When Johnson was enjoying a favorable press, he told a visitor one day, "I trust the press. I trust you just as much as I trust my wife." But when things got bad, he swung to the other side of the scale and exaggerated just as much. "They warp everything I do, they lie about me and about what I do, they don't know the meaning of truth. They are liars and cheats. . . . They behave vulgarly. Photographers are like animals, Rayburn used to say. The press is the least-guided, least-inhibited segment of U.S. society." Yet no sooner had he sketched this bizarre picture than he would again turn around. To an intimate he said that he would grade the press "A minus" as far as his coverage went.

On the stump he was a victim of exaggeration. In the spring of 1966 he flew to Omaha and declared that the tide in the war was beginning to turn. A few days later his assistant Walt Rostow appeared on *Face the Nation* and added that the enemy was "tactically defeated." Johnson came back even stronger, saying at a ranch news conference, "Our diplomatic reports indicate that the opposing forces no longer really expect a military victory in South Vietnam." Vice President Hubert Humphrey tuned up, saying there were "flickering bits of evidence" that Hanoi was wearying of the war. Suddenly a national optimism built up about the war, and Johnson became alarmed and began to blame the press and others for what had occurred. Acting on Johnson's orders, the White House declared that the correspondents had been "mistaking determination for optimism" and that the press had "misinterpreted" the mood of the President. This, of course, was nonsense.

About that same time the President flew to Chicago and fixed his heavy oratory on the critics, declaring, "There will be some nervous Nellies and some who will become frustrated and bothered and break ranks under the strain and some will turn on their leaders, their country and our own fighting men." When there was a great outcry against such an unfair attack on those sincerely troubled by the war, Johnson then launched a campaign to show he was tolerant of dissent—which was highly questionable. The constant swing from extreme to extreme, the persistent exaggeration chipped away at the reliability of the White House word.

The long years in the legislative halls also helped mold Johnson's concept of verity. In some ways the Congress has designed its system to deceive the public. There is the image that is to be presented back home. There is the real image which prevails in the cloakrooms and the secret hideaways under the Capitol dome. Pictures, for instance, are banned in the chambers. Too many voters might get the wrong ideas about the empty seats, or they might see their representatives snoozing or reading a newspaper while others talk. The public, it is reasoned, is not mentally equipped to understand the subtleties that prevail in the great legislative halls. When photographs are taken, it is by express permission of the leadership and they are carefully staged. Johnson himself devoted an entire campaign speech in Newark, New Jersey, to the devious ways of the House. He explained how the Republicans (naturally) took advantage of the system which allows a man to vote at first to kill a bill, then vote to pass it on the final tally, thus being able to tell his constituents that he took either side. In his New Jersey analysis Johnson was ferocious in his exposure of the system, saying, "Fooling the people has become the name of the game for a good many Republicans in Congress. They vote one way on what they call a motion to recommit—that is a highfalutin parliamentary phrase, but I want you folks to get on to it. I am going to take the lid off and let a little light come in. . . . So they know that the motion to recommit a bill is a motion to kill a bill. You can understand that kind of language—a motion to put a dagger in the heart of a bill. . . . But when they came for a final vote on the bill, where you could see what they were doing, half of the Republicans changed from a vote to recommit and voted for passage of the bill. . . . And then they talk about credibility."

The motto on the Hill is "to get along." The Congress members have the privilege of editing their remarks made on the floor. Their eloquence for home consumption becomes exemplary and any fitful passion can be toned down before the public has a chance to look. Smart operators on the Hill often are those who are not pinned down in their beliefs until the last minute and even then they reserve the right to reverse field if circumstances change. One White House aide recalls the meeting of legislative leaders with Johnson when he explained to them what steps he had taken in the Dominican Republic uprising and asked the views (hoping, of course, for endorsement) of the men around the table. Everett Dirksen, the most splendid example of the pure legislative animal, sat directly across from Johnson. When it came his time to speak, he edged forward, as did Johnson, and the two confronted each other across the dark mahogany of the Cabinet table. For fifteen minutes Dirksen talked, taking every possible viewpoint. Few people in the room could discern just what Dirksen's position was. That didn't matter. Johnson understood the old legislative game that was being played. As the mysterious ritual went on, one observer noted that the two participants were in total communication, the rest of the room uncomprehending, Johnson nodding and grunting at the right times. The President knew, as others did not, that Dirksen was behind him but that no remarks he made there would ever be used against him if circumstances changed, because the wily old Republican had invoked the Senate ritual of offering a counter-commitment for every commitment. This, in modified form, was the process which Johnson chose to use on the American people.

Actually, credibility problems had plagued Johnson long before he got to the White House, but at no time were they severe and, indeed, in some ways they enhanced his reputation. There were the stories of his eighty-seven-vote primary victory over Coke Stevenson for the Senate seat in 1948, implying that this margin was possible only because Johnson's political backers had proved more adept at "counting" the votes than had those of Stevenson. A former Johnson aide tells how LBJ as a Senator was pointing out the ramshackle cabin on his Texas ranch which he described in Lincolnesque detail as his birthplace. Johnson's mother was along on the ride, and when her son finished she mildly admonished him, "Why, Lyndon, you know you were born in a much better house closer to town which has been torn down." The listener reports that Johnson replied, "I know, Mama, but everybody has to have a birthplace."

Such accounts about a Congressman or a Senator actually were welcomed. People relished the whiff of wickedness they suggested. Characters were at a premium in the legislative chambers and rogues were sometimes idolized. Besides, in the political world, everything is relative. If Johnson was guilty of some distortion, then his opponents and even his friends were just as guilty.

Johnson's accumulation of many millions of dollars

was another of the things whispered about in the corridors of the Senate. Again, the stories brought as many appreciative chuckles as they did clucks. But there were only very vague rumors and wonderings about how that little Austin radio station KTBC managed to achieve its monopoly position and hold it for twenty years, a veritable financial gusher. Most of the misgivings that might have occurred in some minds gave way, however, to a sort of awe. Buccaneers were part of the Congressional scene—men like Bob Kerr, who candidly confessed he opposed only those deals he was not in on, and Harry Byrd, the Virginian who cloaked with Old Dominion courtliness his own twin empires of politics and finance which merged just across the Potomac.

Senate Majority Leader Lyndon Johnson played the legislative game fiercely, his activities shrouded in mystery, the deals being made in the back rooms. The journalists in the Senate press galleries depended on him for news, convivial company and even the quarters they occupied, so there was no really perceptive reporting until he began to be considered for the Presidency. By and large, he had a worshipful press, and much of it was deserved. His legislative track record in the Senate was the best in history. The minds of many reporters are shaped like box-scores. Numbers in the pigeonholes, denoting bills passed, are what counts—not how you get them there. And Johnson's numbers were staggering.

Johnson was a bargainer. In every transaction, as he saw it, there was something to give and something to be gained. And though he paid lip-service to the pure causes in which men enlist for nothing save the joy of serving, he never did believe that things worked quite so idealistically. A deal must be made. One must maneuver and manage and manipulate. He was absolutely correct in this assumption—in the legislative world. He laid smoke screens. He played his cards close. He held secret meetings. It was a mystic fraternal ritual fully understood only by the brotherhood.

There was sharpened interest in Johnson's credibility when it became obvious in 1960 that he was a candidate for the Democratic nomination. Reporters came away puzzled from long sessions in the Majority Leader's Office in which Johnson would talk about John Kennedy's "rickety little legs," his pallor and obvious poor health. Johnson would produce his own plastic-encased electrocardiogram tracing, which he carried in his wallet, and explain the wiggles as a picture of a perfectly healed heart. Johnson told in contemptuous tones how he had appointed Kennedy to the Foreign Relations Committee at the urging of "his Daddy," Joseph P. Kennedy, who, according to LBJ, called up and pleaded for his little boy. These were amusing stories, particularly the way Johnson told them after several drinks of Cutty Sark Scotch. But as Johnson moved closer to the White House, more and more people began to question these vivid yarns. Yet, once Johnson was made the Vice Presidential nominee, these doubts were pushed back by everyone. Kennedy was the focus of events.

Johnson never changed from legislator to executive. But the Presidency needs candor and constancy. Only so

169

many times can the public be fooled and be forgiving. They are not playing the game like a Senator. They want leadership and not manipulation, or, as one of Johnson's own men lamented, "They want kings and not managers."

Almost at once Johnson's tricky footwork began to erode his credibility. The first and most pressing house-keeping job which Johnson had to do when he became President was finish the preparation of the budget. He undertook it with gusto, having a feel for its impor-tance, particularly with the Senate lions such as Byrd. Johnson, Kennedy and the country had been bracing for a budget that would break $100 billion, a summit of peacetime spending. On December 7 Johnson hinted he couldn't be expected to do any better. He pointed out that Kennedy's budget for that year had been $98.8 billion and there were $3.5 billion of built-in increases. It was New Year's Eve in Texas when Johnson really got down to talk to reporters about money matters. The White House correspondents, as is their custom, chipped in to throw a New Year's party. They assem-bled in Austin's Driskill Hotel, and along toward mid-night the President dropped by. Though the corre-spondents knew that any talk that night was supposed to be off the record, they nevertheless crowded up close to Johnson, asking about the ranch and about his plans for the future. The discussion turned toward the budget. Reporters moved in and out of the inner circle, and I had just sat down for a few minutes of listening. Johnson was very precise about his budget. He explained it all, how the total was expected to be $102 to $103 billion. But he had been working on it, he went on, and he thought he could trim it down some. Somebody asked how much, and he hesitated, fingering his drink, eyes cast down. Speaking in a low voice, he said he might get it down "a billion or two." There was some hasty calculation around the table. Another reporter asked if it would be closer to $101 billion or $100 billion. Again Johnson hesitated, then said, "$100 billion." This was obviously very important news, and despite the approach of New Year's and the tacit off-the-record rule, Johnson was asked if the press could use that figure. He agreed immediately that they could as long as he was not identified as the source. Some of the men filed stories that night. Others waited. It was not long, however, before the new President was being painted as a diligent money-saver who now had the budget down close to $100 billion and would present his handiwork to Congress very soon. A few days later Johnson did present his budget—$97.7 billion dollars. Newsmen were as astonished as others who watch the budget, which can't be too many. But LBJ, at least to some persons, looked like a fiscal wizard. The correspondents, however, who had been writing of his terrible anguish at getting the budget to near $100 billion were not so happy. They felt that they had been deceived, and they had. They felt they had been made a part of some sort of game designed for the greater glory of Lyndon Johnson. They had. On the Hill, with his old journalistic pals, Johnson would have had no trouble.

They would have chuckled and forgotten about it. But the White House is much different. A national budget, while never exactly an honest document, nevertheless is not a plaything. And White House correspondents, despite some of their more cynical moments about the good old American public, keep quite a hard eye on such institutions as the budget. They resented the Johnson game.

Johnson himself gave a clear warning of what was to come. Flying back to Washington from the ranch after the holidays of his first winter as President, LBJ laid out his press doctrine to a group of astonished reporters, including such luminaries as *The New York Times*'s Reston, who had been a ranch guest. In the course of that rambling lecture he declared that it was his desire to "make big men" out of the newsmen who covered him. He would confide in them and treat them as his friends. In return for that, he would expect them to forget certain of his indiscretions and to purposely look the other way when he was doing something that might embarrass him if it showed up in print. It was clearly implied that he wanted them to write their stories as he suggested.

Over the next four years there was a flood of petty deceptions, most of them totally unnecessary. They concerned Johnson's staff appointments and his travels and his routine. He denied one day in his office that he had begun to consider the vacancy on the Supreme Court, created by moving Arthur Goldberg to the United Nations, and the next day he announced the appointment of Abe Fortas. His doctor made a public statement on the excellent state of his health and gave a few details on his daily regimen, including, on Johnson's order, the fact that he drank bourbon. Almost everybody in Washington knew that he had drunk nothing but Cutty Sark Scotch, at least since the time of his heart attack.

He went into the hospital for removal of his gall bladder, assuring everybody that gallstones were his only malady. After the surgery it was revealed that a kidney stone had been removed as well. When it was reported he would ask for a $4-billion cut in excise taxes, the White House claimed the figure was wrong. Later Johnson asked for a cut of $3.9 billion. LBJ denied a story he would seek a three-percent Federal pay raise, then he did just that. Johnson berated the press for misinforming the readers that Texas State Democratic Chairman Marvin Watson would join his White House staff. Watson, of course, was recruited. When he read a news leak that he intended to appoint Deputy Under Secretary of State U. Alexis Johnson his ambassador to Japan, a furious LBJ horned in on a news conference being conducted by Secretary of Agriculture Orville Freeman and implied that it was all false by scornfully saying the report was "some kid's statement over at the State Department." There was a double credibility score on that one. Not only was Alexis Johnson later appointed ambassador, but when the official transcript of the incident was issued the crucial language was changed to read "someone's statement over at the State Department." Johnson was even capable of a triple play. He told some visitors that he intended to name Negro Walter Washington to a high post in the District of Columbia government, which he was revising. After a newspaper reported that Washington was to be D.C.'s new mayor, Johnson passed the word that he would not appoint him after all. Johnson, looking as if he had dined on a large helping of crow, eventually summoned reporters to the Cabinet Room and named Washington mayor.

Johnson thought he might take a short campaign swing early in the fall of 1966, talking to the steelworkers in Atlantic City, the carpenters in Kansas City and the electrical workers in St. Louis. The mayors of those cities were alerted, the local security forces put on notice. When news stories that the President was expected came out of those cities, he grew angry and called the talks off. The White House denied that Johnson had ever intended to go, invoking the technicality that he had not finally said "yes." A host of angry civic and labor leaders were simply ignored.

When the Bobby Baker scandal broke, Johnson took great pains to try to convince his listeners that Baker had not been a "protégé of mine." It was a preposterous assumption that past history could be blotted out simply by denying it. Baker *was* Johnson's protégé—indeed, was the aide closest to Johnson on the Hill.

Asked if he was looking for a successor to Ambassador Henry Cabot Lodge in Vietnam, Johnson replied at a news conference, "No, there is no truth that I am looking for a successor." A week later Ellsworth Bunker was appointed to the job and Press Secretary George Christian sickly explained, "The President was not 'looking' for a successor because he had already found him." The White House insisted that no announcement about the proposed supersonic transport plane was imminent. Next day the Federal Aviation Agency announced that Boeing had been selected to build the airframe.

By themselves these things were only passing irritants in the daily Washington world. But their accumulation was another matter. They created a miasma of doubt that found its way into the writings of reporters and then commentators. The reporters on the White House beat were the first to know what was happening. About a year later the pundits such as Lippmann and Reston sensed the problem. The public lagged behind even then, but after only two years most of the nation had the same uneasy feeling that newsmen had sensed on New Year's Eve of 1964.

The counselors of Johnson propounded a theory about Johnson as the protest began to mount. They agreed that on small matters he was careless, imprecise, impetuous. But on the large matters, the ones that really counted, he was cool, calm and candid. For a few months it appeared to be true that Johnson could somehow divide himself in his daily routine, be outrageous in trivia but rational on major matters. Some thoughtful men doubted that in the long run the two Johnsons could be held apart or at least be distinguished by the people.

Almost all of Johnson's major speeches, his messages

175

to Congress and other principal statements, were straightforward at first. But then on some problems of great significance the symptoms of deception began to appear.

In the fall of 1965, when aluminum producers announced a price increase that would have serious effects on the economy which Johnson was skillfully managing to record-breaking heights, the government suddenly announced that it was dumping on the market some 200,000 tons of stockpiled aluminum, a ploy which successfully battered the prices back into line. When the White House was asked if there was a connection between the dumping and the price hike—a *pro forma* question since the government action was obviously designed to counter the price increase—there was the shocking response: "No connection whatsoever." Beyond that, newsmen were assured privately that the White House had not been deeply involved in the price fight and the President had had nothing to do with it. This flimsy veil lasted only momentarily. Very shortly Johnson boasted to his friends of his role in winning the price roll-back and told how he personally had talked to a senior executive of Alcoa. Most observers were again perplexed as to why the White House felt it was necessary to deny the President's involvement. Perhaps he worried that the display of the government strong arm might alienate some of his business supporters. But the business community has a superb grapevine and all the important executives knew almost instantly of Johnson's role. Further, had the President actually not gotten involved in the pricing war, a rather good case could have been made that he was not performing his Presidential duties. The aluminum incident set off very serious doubts about Johnson's credibility among businessmen who up until then had been among his staunch supporters.

Even earlier that same year the close students of foreign policy were alarmed by Johnson's torrent of explanations on why he had sent 24,000 troops into the Dominican Republic. Johnson was criticized harshly for dispatching such a large force to that small country. It was the most severe battering he had received on his international decisions, and he was understandably sensitive about it. His reaction was to spend literally hours with reporters and guests going over, detail by detail, his reasons for sending the large number of troops. On the Saturday when he talked almost continuously for seven hours with aides and newsmen, he repeatedly brought up the Dominican matter. He could not forget it. He spent three hours at lunch with a clutch of magazine reporters, pacing back and forth, telling in excruciating detail why he had done what he had done. The more he talked, however, the more the story ceased to resemble the facts. The first White House explanation for the troops was that they were there to protect the lives of the two thousand Americans living in the Dominican Republic. Johnson then changed his story and said that the U.S. intervention was to prevent a communist takeover. Nobody worried much about that. It is perfectly reasonable for the government to counter communism under the guise of protecting American lives. Few people had any doubts about our real reasons for being in Santo Domingo. The question was simply about the size of the force, which to that small country—and to all of Latin America—looked like the Yankee hordes come for conquest. Johnson brooded in private as long as he could, and then he burst forth in June of 1965 with some astounding hyperbole. "Some fifteen hundred innocent people were murdered and shot, and their heads cut off, and . . . as we talked to our Ambassador to confirm the horror and tragedy and the unbelievable fact that they were firing on Americans and the American embassy, he was talking to us from under a desk while bullets were going through his windows, and he had a thousand American men, women and children assembled in the hotel who were pleading with their President for help to preserve their lives." No one was beheaded, only a few American troops were shot by the insurgents. Ambassador W. Tapley Bennett, Jr., later couldn't remember any bullets coming through his windows and he had not hidden under his desk. Ironically, the Dominican intervention was one of Johnson's most successful foreign-policy ventures. Quick action and firmness and then patience as Ellsworth Bunker helped guide the country back to stability paid off handsomely. It is reasonable from this distance to assume that if Johnson had simply explained that his dispatch of troops was not only to protect Americans but also to prevent another Castro in Latin America, there would have been a minimum of criticism. The incident now has become one of the prize specimens in the showcase of "incredibility," the word Johnson uses when he talks of the problem.

The Vietnam war, because of its complexity and its horror, naturally became a part of the Administration's believability problem from the start. On that matter Johnson has been treated unfairly. He has been constantly reminded of statements he made about Vietnam when conditions there were of one nature, and these have been compared to his actions later when conditions changed dramatically. Johnson matched the U.S. war effort to that of the aggressors. His critics insisted unfairly that he abide by his early doctrine.

Johnson's campaign dialogue through the fall of 1964 is often regurgitated in this careless attack on him. He called the idea of enlarging the American part in the war "reckless action" that might threaten the peace of the world. He declared that it was an "illusion" that force, or the threat of force, could resolve the problems there. "Before I start dropping bombs around the country, I would want to think about the consequences of getting American boys into a war with seven hundred million Chinese," he said. The fact is that Johnson believed what he said. The situation which he analyzed did not call for further American involvement. His private talk was much the same as that on the stump. Riding his big jet back and forth across the nation, he counseled those in his plane about the total instability of the Saigon government and about how dangerous further United States commitment would be. He recalled the counsel of General Douglas MacArthur not to get into a war on the Asian mainland, and his own observations of that teeming place, gleaned from his Vice Presidential trip, led him to the same conviction.

Johnson's enemy was his overstatement, not his lack of truth in these matters. He believed what he said—for that moment. But a President should understand that conditions in such fertile revolutionary ground as South Vietnam can change with frightening speed. A politician of Johnson's stripe should know that hyperbole is dangerous. There was no stopping him that fall, however. The world was his and the polls showed it.

More serious charges about Johnson's war credibility arose later. He denied obvious changes in policy. It can be argued, and *was* argued by the White House, that shifts in the intensity of our operations were not "policy" changes. But these were arguments too delicate for most people to appreciate, and they were on the borderline of deception. When Johnson first ordered sustained bombing north of the 17th Parallel, newsmen were routed out of bed to be told that the planes had attacked an ammunition dump at Dong Hoi, North Vietnam. In almost the same breath the White House denied this was escalation of the war, insisting it was a "reprisal" raid in answer to the mortar attack on the American barracks at Pleiku. Strategy had not been changed, only tactics. As the American troops expanded in number and were committed to combat, a conflicting welter of explanations came from White House, State Department and Defense Department. At first it was denied that American Marines had a combat mission. Then it was acknowledged from Saigon and the State Department. This infuriated Johnson, who had it explained that General William Westmoreland had had the authority to commit the troops to combat from the start. Johnson seemed, in his great anguish at having to assume the brunt of the war, to want to delay the impact on the American people as long as possible, to be trying to screen what was really happening so that the public could quietly assimilate it and not really protest. He was, once again, trying to create a false impression for a given moment in history, believing that his cause and eventually that of the nation would benefit.

One of Johnson's Cabinet officers who had fought loyally through the credibility war nearly gave up when Johnson returned from his Asian tour in October of 1966 and denied that he had planned to go campaigning for Democratic Senators and Congressmen who were in deep political trouble that off-year. During the Asian tour Bill Moyers had alerted reporters that upon returning to the mainland the President would make a four-day, fifteen-state airborne political assault. Secret Service agents and advance men already had spread out over the land and were readying things for the President. The big-city mayors, like Richard Daley of Chicago, had passed the good word to their loyalists and the parade routes were planned, the stands built, the bands hired. The local papers bannered these preparations. An amused and expectant citizenry braced for a

Johnson in seven-league boots, fresh from his Asian success. But, once back in the White House, Johnson announced at a news conference that his only trip would be to his ranch to rest for surgery involving the removal of a throat polyp and an incisional hernia which had erupted from his gall-bladder operation. The plans for campaigning, he suggested, had been imagined. "The people," he told the news conference, "ought to know that all these canceled plans primarily involve the imagination of people who phrase sentences and write columns and have to report what they hope or what they imagine." Johnson's aides and his principal Cabinet officers were disheartened. "That proved," said one weary Cabinet officer, "everything they had been saying about Johnson's credibility." Bill Moyers had worked out a careful answer for Johnson on that particular question so that the disappointed politicians would know why he had to change plans. But Johnson discarded it. Something happened, as it did frequently, when he got in front of the microphones and reporters began to prod him about something he did not want to discuss. His fear of openness arose. His resentment at others dispelling the secrecy which he considered essential for effective action overwhelmed his better judgment.

In trying to justify that phenomenon, Moyers and others explained that "premature disclosure reduces the President's options. Fundamental to his operations and way of life is surprise, which keeps his foes off balance. He wants to retain the advantage of calling his own signals and deciding on his own timing." Thus, Johnson became obsessed with news leaks, became outraged when his plans were divulged by someone else. The "open option" theory is feasible and perhaps even necessary in legislative matters. But essentially the United States is not an open-option nation. It is an ordered society, based on advanced planning. Industrialists must commit themselves to courses of action months ahead of time. Workers must plan their lives around strict schedules, rigid down to hours and days. The luxury of deciding an issue in the last minute is reserved for only a few. The privilege to rush off across the country on an impulse or to cancel such a trip in the same way is rare. Johnson as a legislator liked to live that way and did. A President can ill afford such erratic action. He is the symbol, and in this society it is imperative that he be reasonably predictable and constant. Johnson's reluctance to conform deepened the credibility problem.

Indeed, as the little credibility violations accumulated and the larger incidents multiplied, a great many Johnson mannerisms and methods began to contribute to the rising tide of disbelief and uncertainty. In just about everything Johnson did, overtones of the central credibility problem were noted. When *Life,* after thorough and painstaking research (with no help from Johnson), estimated the President's fortune at $14 million, there was a struggle before the article was published to get it dropped or revised. *Life* editors were alternately appealed to and argued with in a long night session which included the family attorney, Abe Fortas. Johnson seemed afraid of the fact that he had become so wealthy. *Life,* of course, went ahead. Johnson's response was a careful accountant's statement of his holdings which put his worth at $3.4 million. The figure was meaningless, since it was based on the purchase price of Johnson's holdings, which bore no relationship to the market value some fifteen years after the property was acquired. It was all very prim and very legal. It just gave a totally misleading picture. And most people knew it. As Johnson rode with some ranch guests through downtown Johnson City in 1967, one of his companions remarked that the small town must have benefited from Johnson's Presidency and be enjoying an economic boom. Johnson quickly denied it, pointing out that "the population was six hundred when I was a boy, is about the same now." He was apparently fearful that someone might suspect he was benefiting from the increase in town business and corresponding rise in values, and so he chose to deny the facts which were plainly visible on both sides of the street down which he was driving. Johnson City's Mayor George Byars proudly and consistently burbled his delight at the new boom.

Once the President made a big speech to those around him about how he had checked up and found out that every time he traveled he uprooted seven hundred people. He was going to stay at the White House and work, he declared. Johnson then proceeded to become the most traveled President of the postwar years.

He explained in detail his trips to the Texas ranch, pointing out that he could work much better down there, away from the ceremonial duties and out of reach of a lot of the unimportant phone calls. But when his popularity fell and the opinion samplers found that some people did not like the fact that he spent so much time at his ranch, he quickly shifted ground and remained for a few weeks at the White House, explaining, "Here's where my work is."

For a while he urged reporters to call him up if they had questions. If all the newsmen he had suggested that to had called him, he would have had no time for anything else. Correspondents knew that. *The New York Times*'s Charles Mohr thought he would test it once. He called to talk to the President and after a long wait finally got Bill Moyers and explained that Johnson had urged him to phone. After another wait the President came on the line and said, "I told you that you could visit me, but I didn't say you could move in with me."

Johnson seemed to feel at first a sense of protection in the Presidency which lured him into compromising situations. When he drove at high speeds over the Texas state highways with a cup of beer and passed on a hill, he reasoned that because the fifty or so reporters who knew about the incident (some of whom were in his car with him) were his ranch guests, they would respect the confidence. When the stories broke, he angrily denied them and then, seeing that was unsuccessful, he bitterly attacked the publications which reported and printed the accounts. It was hard to tell from that incident whether he hurt himself more by the denials of fact or by the example of law-breaking.

The President constantly indulged in small image-building rituals that were unnecessary and emerged as "too cute." When stories were written that he looked tired or that he had not been seen for several days, he would appear at odd moments putting on a display of physical vigor—traveling, working all night, walking— to show that he never got tired, a ridiculous claim to indestructibility. Sometimes he suddenly would show up in the press lobby, then stride out the front door, down Pennsylvania Avenue and back into the White House. He would explain he just wanted fresh air, but always these minidramas occurred when someone had raised the question of his well-being. At World Series time he dropped by the White House pressroom, ob- viously to show the world that he, too, was a baseball fan, and he stood with reporters for five minutes in the midst of one of the 1967 games. But he hardly looked at the TV screen and did not even inquire about the score. Johnson never seemed to sense that a President did not have to make excuses about how he occupied his time nor did he need to embellish the drama of the Presi- dency. It was intense enough.

When Johnson was high in the polls, he could not talk about them enough. "The reason I love so many polls is that over the years I've learned that they're pretty accurate, that they tell pretty well what's going on," he said. When his polls plummeted, he changed his assessment. The polls became less important. He told his visitors then that they were not always accurate, and he began to talk more about the private findings of his partisans who brought news that contradicted the professional samplers. This was a very human reaction and probably would have been excused had not the credibility weight been hanging around his neck. In that context, his variable assessment of polls contributed to the credibility gap.

Credibility was assaulted by the atmosphere of unreality that Johnson's men created around him. Marvin Watson as late as January of 1968 still practiced his unskilled political intrigue. He assembled and instructed lesser White House aides to go to the House well for Johnson's State of the Union Address and to lead the applause and cheering at certain crucial points. It was a gross insult to the Congress and, indeed, to the Presidency, a thought that apparently never coursed through Watson's literal mind.

The well-meaning Jack Valenti, in sincere ardor for the man he worked for, perhaps did as much as anybody to make people begin to wonder about the improbable world of LBJ. Speaking before the Advertising Federation of America in Boston in June 1965, Valenti created some startling verbal images. He described Johnson as "a sensitive man, a cultivated man, a warm-hearted and extraordinary man." The enraptured Valenti suggested that the President got something extra through a process he called "Godly osmosis" and he went on to say that Johnson, "thank the good Lord, has extra glands." He called the Presidency "a sky-tall summit" and proceeded in some singularly textured English to say: "The Presidency is a mystical body, constructed by the Constitution, but whose architecture was conceived in the inner crannies of a people's soul. . . . An odd mixture of royal divinity and equalitarian choice—a union between a nation yearning for continuity and its firm resolve not to yield one jot of independence." To Valenti, Johnson loomed as solid and imposing as a "large gray stone mountain." And finally there was the line that fixed itself in the Johnsonian history: "I sleep each night a little better, a little more confidently, because Lyndon Johnson is my President. For I know he lives and thinks and works to make sure that for all America and indeed, the growing body of the free world, the morning shall always come."

Even as the credibility problem deepened, Johnson could not break himself of his habits. He persisted in staging his playlets, and almost always they backfired. After an agonizing three months of searching for a new Under Secretary of State, he made a surprise announcement at one of his office news conferences. In an "oh, by the way" manner in answer to a question by the St. Louis *Post-Dispatch*'s Marquis Childs, he said he had decided that Attorney General Nicholas de B. Katzenbach was to be the man. When some writers criticized the President for such a casual approach to such an important announcement, he got terribly defensive. He denied that he had planned it that way, a denial that was patently false since Childs had been told by State

Department aides to ask the question and, indeed, Bob Fleming, Assistant Press Secretary, fearing that the question would not be asked as the press conference went on, had scribbled the key question on a note pad and was ready to pass it to a reporter so LBJ could spring his surprise. Caught once again, LBJ spent long evening hours trying, as he had with the Dominican Republic intervention, to sell the unsalable explanation that he had not wanted to make the announcement in that manner but had decided only on the spur of the moment to do it. Even if the story were true, which it was not, an Under Secretary of State is a vital personality in foreign affairs and such pedestrian treatment of his appointment could not enhance his prestige.

Another of Johnson's peccadillos which enlarged the credibility gap was his habit of frequently changing the ground rules without telling those with whom he was dealing. At Johnson's request, Walter Heller, then chairman of the Council of Economic Advisors, invited former chairmen of the CEA in 1965 to meet secretly at the White House with the President and discuss the need for a tax increase. Heller in his invitations was careful to point out that their remarks were to be held in confidence. Johnson found, in the course of the meeting, that the six men around him were in general agreement with his economic approach. He was naturally pleased. Unexpectedly, he asked if it was all right to call in the press and have the men make a statement. Not wishing to offend the President, the stunned group acquiesced. Heller, embarrassed but not wanting to counter Johnson, drafted a statement with the help of the visiting economists. The press was notified, pictures were taken and Johnson chortled the good news that these men stood behind him. The illusion lasted only as long as it took these economists to get back to their offices. *The New York Times* reported the story as it appeared at the White House. *Time* magazine's Juan Cameron called the participants and got irritated contradictions. Shortly after that, a worried and wounded Walter Heller left the government to return to the campus of the University of Minnesota.

Johnson compounded his troubles because of his naïveté as to how the Washington press corps operated— this after thirty-six years in the city. He was, strangely, an alien in the journalistic thicket. He did not comprehend the camaraderie of reporters, or their conviction that virtually everything said in and around Washington—whether in one's home or on the street—somehow bore on the public's business and was, at one time or another, for use. Kennedy, with many fewer years in Washington, knew this. "I figure," said JFK one time, "that whenever I talk with reporters on background I am talking for the record sooner or later." In one of his early press backgroundings, rambling around the South Lawn of the White House, Johnson explained in his most colorful style the very logical reasons he had asked that the visits of India's Shastri and Pakistan's Ayub Khan be postponed. The postponements had created quite a diplomatic stir, but Johnson had good reasons, wanting to see what Congress did with his foreign-aid request before he talked to the two men. In his graphic way the President explained that both countries, because they had been critical of our involvement in Vietnam, were in some disfavor in the U.S. Congress. He embellished it by saying that their coming at that time was like having your mother-in-law arrive when you had tickets to the ballgame. It took only about an hour for this spicy account to rush through the halls of the National Press Building. George Reedy soon had pop-eyed Asian correspondents in his office demanding to know what Johnson had said, and the episode clattered around the world in wild exaggerations.

Johnson seemed incapable of changing, so deeply ingrained was his feeling of omnipotence. When the *Sun's* Potter dug out a story that the President was prepared to disclose a new Food for Peace program which would require buying food on the open market since United States surpluses were diminished, Johnson felt betrayed, and instead of going ahead with his plans he ordered the mimeographed releases burned and camouflaged his plans in piecemeal announcements so that he could deny the accuracy of Potter's account. In such incidents the back offices of the White House and related agencies were terrorized as Johnson launched investigations to see who had leaked the stories. And, of course, when the Administration officers were asked if Johnson really had altered his plans because of news leaks, there were heated denials. Then, in this thicket of inconsistency, Johnson admitted it was true. In the fall of 1966 at an open press conference Johnson lectured reporters on the evils of speculative journalism. "When you see on the ticker that Oshkosh says that Bob Pierpoint (the CBS reporter who had questioned Johnson) may be named Chairman of the Joint Chiefs of Staff you don't necessarily give much credence to it, because the very fact that it is on there is the best indication that it is not likely to happen."

As the 1968 election approached, Johnson seemed mired in this terrible swamp. The testimony of Press Secretary Number Four, George Christian, on a nationwide radio show, that the President was "a very candid man" who is "rather open in his discussions with the press and with the public" became a credibility cause in itself. When fifty thousand peace marchers descended on Washington, the White House put out an elaborate and patently phony schedule of Johnson's activities that weekend in an effort to show that the President was too busy to pay heed to the marchers. LBJ posed for pictures in the Rose Garden with visitors, and reporters were counseled in detail on his Saturday duties, a departure from the normal Saturday somnolence at 1600 Pennsylvania Avenue. All of it was too contrived to be believed. And it was unnecessary. The President of the United States did not have to make excuses for ignoring such a gathering of rabble. At about the same time the governors were aboard the U.S.S. *Independence* sailing for the Virgin Islands and the great debate on shipboard and in Washington was whether the governors would pass a resolution of support for Johnson's Vietnam policy as they had done the two previous years.

Publicly, George Christian denied that the President was making any attempt to get such a resolution. Privately, Christian told select newsmen that Johnson was keeping his hands off. Only hours later Ronald Reagan had a copy of a cable from Johnson's Special Assistant, Marvin Watson, outlining to Price Daniel, Director of the Office of Defense Mobilization and a Johnson political operative, the strategy for wringing such a resolution from the governors. Christian hurriedly apologized to those reporters he had misled. But the damage was done. Whether the Press Secretary knew the facts or not did not matter. The instructions must have come from the President, since Watson had neither the background nor the authority to act on his own. The purloined cable, which would have been an acceptable part of any President's political defenses in a terribly difficult period, became yet another manifestation of the incredibility of Lyndon B. Johnson.

His great round-the-world peace mission the week before Christmas in 1967 was conceived in secrecy. The advance party was sent to Rome to arrange a meeting with the Pope on Christmas Eve. The American embassy was not told. Johnson wanted to swoop down out of the sky and hold a historic conference. To confide in the embassy or the Italian government would produce premature stories for such an extravaganza. The advance party sneaked into Rome and took rooms in a downtown hotel. The White House switchboard did not know their whereabouts, so called Ambassador Frederick Reinhardt every half-hour through one night.

By morning he began to get the picture and he was upset at being bypassed. The Vatican, meantime, insisted that the President call on the Italian government, which had learned about the visit by that time and was also angry. Johnson, hurtling around the world on his jet, tried desperately to maintain the fiction that he did not know whether he would stop in Rome or not. That was one of those technical truths because final agreement was not reached until he was a few hours out of Rome. The fact, however, was that he desperately wanted the meeting with the Pope and had planned it for days, but because of that strange inner compulsion to keep his plans secret he launched the elaborate deception which in the end caused more trouble than if he had been candid.

Credibility became the single biggest problem in Lyndon Johnson's four years of leadership. It tainted in some way almost everything else he did. In a vague way he sensed the problem, particularly when it began to show up in the national polls. Louis Harris found in his sampling early in 1967 that the people's personal confidence in the President was about twenty points below their ratings of him on the conduct of the office of the Presidency and his management of the war. Johnson at first blamed the press. "I never used to have trouble with the press," he lamented to a friend one night. "I don't understand it." Before his popularity dropped below a majority, he could even joke about it. But it became increasingly difficult for anybody to get much humor from the problem. On one evening stroll the

President wondered aloud, "Why should Ho Chi Minh believe me when the newspapers and the networks in my own country don't believe me?" There was no indication that he felt himself responsible for the situation, but he was feeling the effect in his conduct of the country's affairs.

OCCURRENCE

THE FIRST word of the Middle East crisis came to the White House Situation Room shortly before three a.m. Walt Rostow was sleeping soundly at his home when his phone rang and one of those anonymous government voices said matter-of-factly, "We have a FBIS [Foreign Broadcasting Information Service] that the U.A.R. has launched an attack on Israel."

In his years at the vortex of power Rostow has developed a crisis response, a physical and mental conditioning for the inevitable hours of stress that will follow. His chemistry changed almost automatically. He told his caller to check other intelligence sources. In a few minutes the man called back and said that all the reports were the same. "Okay," answered Rostow, "I'm coming in." He shaved quickly, but did not bother about breakfast. A White House limousine sped him through the silent Washington streets as he made mental calculations about his procedure.

By 3:25 he was in the Situation Room pouring over the cables. They told of air-raid sirens heard in Cairo and Tel Aviv. There were fragmentary facts on the locations of tanks. Most important were notations that some of the Arab airfields seemed inoperative, indicating a strong Israeli air strike.

Rostow called Rusk and found that he knew and was watching too. They agreed that if the information continued to support their initial conclusions Rostow should awaken the President at 4:30. The trickle of facts began to swell. It was certain—there was war. Rostow picked up the white phone that sits on a plain table in the Situation Room beneath the harsh glare of neon lights. "I want to get through to the President," he said. "I wish him to be awakened." At Johnson's bedside a phone rang softly—just loud enough to wake the President.

"Yes," said Johnson.

"Mr. President," Rostow said, "This is Walt. I have the following to report. We have information that Israel and the U.A.R. are at war." Johnson said nothing for a few seconds as Rostow raced on with the facts he had. Johnson asked for more information and told Rostow to make certain that our ambassadors were doing everything they could to protect United States citizens. He asked other questions that launched him into potentially the most explosive situation he had yet faced. Where were the forces? Who was involved? How had it started? He put the phone down and catnapped the night out.

In the Situation Room the tempo increased. A coffee urn bubbled and the staff sent out for rolls, since the White House mess had not opened. Clark Clifford, head of Johnson's Foreign Intelligence Advisory Board, came in. Press Secretary George Christian and his assistant, Tom Johnson, hurried across the Potomac as dawn broke. LBJ woke and called both Rusk and McNamara.

About eight a.m. the most startling news of all clattered in over the wire. The hot line was being activated by Moscow. A Russian translator was summoned. Johnson was phoned again. Still in his bedroom, he listened. His expression did not change as he said to Christian, "Let's go to the Situation Room." When he arrived the first message from Alexei Kosygin was rolling off on the yellow cable paper, a plea for restraint, the beginning of a historic and cooling dialogue in the white heat of war.

COMMAND

THE COMMANDER-IN-CHIEF is a paradox. Lyndon B. Johnson runs a war machine that he basically distrusts and dislikes, and with it he fights a war that he hates. At the same time he is deeply concerned that his courage might be questioned or that his resolve might be found wanting in the pages of history. The United States course in the Vietnam war is a product of these crosscurrents. On the one hand he anguishes over the billions of dollars that are going for bombs instead of being used in building this country—and his own legend—and on the other hand he is fearful that a Texan, nurtured in the idiom of the Rangers, might be called a coward. Johnson is never at ease in the epicenter of these forces. He has sought a middle ground where he might momentarily be comfortable, but it has proved terribly elusive.

LBJ's great, glimmering dreams, which only a boy from the Texas Hill Country reared on James Whitcomb Riley could concoct, were of a Presidency that would joyously pursue the millennium, and, to hear

Johnson tell it, that golden age was only a pant or two away. Bombs and bullets were anathema to the President. His wars were to be against heart disease and cancer. He rallied his forces to smite poverty and ignorance. The intrusion of a real shooting war was a crushing blow to him. He protested at first. He wanted to hold to his dream and fight the war as a sideline. He was certain—and the economic figures bore him out—that this country could have both bullets and butter, but he failed to calculate the American mentality, a mistake he made more than once. The people were just not fully at ease with themselves in all their prosperity while some of their sons died in the muck of South Vietnam. Johnson, as usual, was good at the figures. The $30 billion a year which the war cost was only about 4 percent of the gross national product—hardly a noticeable strain on the surging economy. The stress showed up in the hearts of the people, who anguished increasingly about our proper role in the world and, of course, about the destruction and the killing on both sides. This kind of psychological computation, however, was not one of Johnson's talents. He dreaded the battle casualties as much as anyone, but he could not communicate his reasoning behind the war. It was perhaps inevitable under those circumstances that he eventually was branded by extremists as some kind of crazed bomber or, even worse, a man under the spell of the generals. That was nonsense.

He himself protested vehemently in private about such an assessment. Accused of not paying attention to

the so-called "peace feelers," which, indeed, were sub-
stanceless flurries, he raged, "Do they think that I'm
some kind of war villain or an idiot who can't read an
English sentence?" During a bombing pause he received
a call from an influential Senator who offered some
pointed military advice. "Mr. President," said the
caller, "you've got to resume the bombing of North
Vietnam. You've got to win this thing now. You've got
to go for the jugular. I urge you to turn this war over to
your military commanders. They are the men who
know how to wage war, and they will win it." Johnson
did not hesitate in his answer. "Not as long as I am
President. As long as I sit here, the control will stay
with the Commander-in-Chief." The Senator persisted:
"We've got to win it. . . . That's why Roosevelt and
Truman were so great. They let their military leaders
do the job." Again Johnson had an answer. "I was
around in those days," he said. "There were not many
decisions made that Roosevelt did not know about. And
Harry Truman watched everything closely. . . . I'm not
going to let the hounds loose." Though Johnson was
never intrigued with military science, he was certain of
the wisdom of civil control in waging war. While he did
not meddle in strategy and tactics, the President set the
size of the war which we were to fight.

His deep suspicions of the military went back to his
first days in the Congress. When he came to Washington
in 1937, because of his loyalty to Roosevelt and because
rising Congressman Sam Rayburn was his friend, he
was given a seat on Carl Vinson's powerful Naval Af-

fairs Committee. There he watched the high brass parade, and he was disturbed. He found that too many military men grew arrogant behind the ribbons they wore on their chests. He found them often contemptuous of new ideas, mean and thoughtless in dealing with those below them. He detected an alarming amount of sheer stupidity which was self-perpetuating because of the academy caste system. He found no companionship among military men. Philosophically, he found nothing in their repertoires to enchant him. Johnson was occupied with bringing the twentieth century to his poor Texas district, and the very thought of spending huge sums on weapons when the rivers of Central Texas still ravaged the countryside after every heavy rain and then a few months later the land shriveled because of lack of water was depressing to Congressman Johnson. Yet, when war came to Europe, the agile-minded Johnson was in the vanguard—even ahead of some of the top brass—in calling for American preparedness. In fact, the general level of competence which Johnson found among the admirals who came before the Naval Affairs Committee convinced him that the nation could not put its complete trust in the military in such hazardous times. How America met the threat had to be planned in detail, in Johnson's view, by the politicians.

This lack of confidence in the officer corps never really left Johnson. Certainly he made individual friends in the services through the years. And as President he was just as lavish in his praise of such men as

General Earle Wheeler, Chairman of the Joint Chiefs, and General William Westmoreland, his commander in Vietnam, as he was of anybody else. But quite correctly he felt that the military men almost always were too narrow in their appraisals of a given problem, often ignoring the political implications in the United States or the reaction abroad. Long years of peacetime service with unparalleled resources to build the mightiest military machine in history had made the Pentagon warriors too often insensitive to the delicate feelings that accompanied the wave of the new freedom which swept around the globe. Johnson could be merciless when he told about the generals. None got harsher treatment than the old bomber pilot Curt LeMay, chief of the Air Force under Kennedy and Johnson. LeMay was credited with having offered the advice for the air war in North Vietnam, "We ought to bomb them back to the stone age." LBJ remembered with particular contempt a budget-making session held by President Kennedy in Palm Beach. LeMay insisted that a certain multimillion-dollar item had been left out of the budget (implying civil subterfuge) and it was essential for the Air Force. Secretary of Defense McNamara calmly told the General that he was mistaken and if he would look on such-and-such a page he would find the funds he was worried about. Unbelieving, LeMay fastened on his spectacles, turned to the designated page, read the item, and then, as Johnson recounted the incident, "looked up just like he had been hit in the face with a sack of shit." Later that day when Kennedy ordered a break in the budget deliberations for a swim in the pool, he splashed over to Johnson's side and said, "It certainly is a good thing the founding fathers placed the military under civilian control." Johnson subscribed heartily to an axiom that Kennedy propounded before his death. One night in his office with friends, JFK said, "Once you decide to send the bombers, you want men like LeMay flying them. But you can't let them decide if they should go or not."

Johnson did not even share Kennedy's fascination with the tools and techniques of war. Kennedy loved to review the men, and at least twice a year he took excursions into the field or out with the fleet. He watched maneuvers in both Atlantic and Pacific, witnessed B52's scramble and heard the attack planes crack the sound barrier. He reviewed miles of infantry ranks, watched Marines storm a beach and counter-insurgents parachute into a lake. He chuckled over judo demonstrations and watched an Atlas shoot at Vandenberg Air Force Base. Johnson never bothered with such missions until he had been President almost two years and the involvement in the Vietnam war made it politically necessary that he take an interest.

When conducting the war became the major occupation of the White House and Johnson established the Tuesday luncheon for his top national-security deliberations, it was notable that at first no military man was regularly included. The group was composed of Secretaries Rusk and McNamara, Special Assistant Walt Rostow and, at first, Press Secretary Bill Moyers, later replaced by George Christian. This was without any doubt, during the eighteen months in which it functioned in that intimate form, the most powerful policy-making group in the Administration. Not only were long-range plans developed, but the smallest of details sometimes came up. One day, as Johnson hunched over the targeting maps which had been brought by McNamara, the final decisions might be made on where and how to bomb next. The following week this group might be discussing the state of mind of Red China, and at the next meeting they might dwell for a moment on the scrambled eggs which were supplied the men in the foxholes. Johnson felt that the consultative process was thorough enough that all the military thoughts worthy of attention were brought to the Tuesday luncheon by McNamara, who was the man designated to speak for the entire defense establishment. The military men had their say at National Security Council meetings. They could seek audiences with the President whenever they wanted. And when special questions came up concerning Vietnam, Johnson would ask them to dine. Nevertheless, in the spring of 1967 when Johnson's popularity with the people dropped to new lows and dissent from both right and left built up on the Hill, one of the issues which was pursued by the critics was Johnson's failure to heed the advice of the military. One high general late at night in a Washington men's club told a disturbed group around him that the NSC session seemed more an occasion for issuing orders to the military, or at least for informing them of decisions that had been made, than a deliberative affair where alternative actions were weighed and diverse voices listened to. When a series of military men began to complain to John Stennis' Armed Services Committee and when Stennis himself objected that too much military advice was being ignored, Johnson abruptly altered the format of his consultations. General Wheeler was included in more of the vital sessions, and other generals and admirals were brought to the White House with more regularity. Yet that hardly changed Johnson's approach or, really, his attitude toward the military. More visible consultation calmed the critics, but Johnson went right on taking the crucial measure of events with his four or five most trusted civilians.

"All those generals want to do," he once said, "is bomb and spend." Nor could Johnson get used to the fact that frequently things went wrong in the field. The inaccuracy of the aerial war was particularly perplexing to him, and one afternoon in the Oval Room he told an audience of newsmen that he had asked the Air Force to choose the most accurate bombardiers for one of the first missions against North Vietnam. He was too familiar, he said, with how planes could be sent to attack a target and have their bombs land a hundred miles away. When the first strike against the petroleum supplies was ordered, Johnson worried a good many hours, as he said later, about having a bomb fall down the smokestack of one of the Russian ships in the Haiphong harbor. "It would be my luck," he told amused guests, "to have the plane which drops the bomb on a Russian ship which starts World War III piloted by a boy from Johnson City whose family were friends of my Daddy's."

There was always one exception to Lyndon Johnson's skepticism about the military mentality. That was Dwight D. Eisenhower. There were some obvious reasons why Johnson would repeatedly tell his intimates, "Eisenhower is the best general that I've ever known anything about." He frequently sought and got Ike's advice on the full range of Presidential problems, and in most cases he got the former President's endorsement, which was a political bonus worth having. Johnson deserved such treatment from Ike, since, as Majority Leader, LBJ many times stood behind the Republican. But beyond that Johnson sincerely admired Ike's ability to harmonize divergent views and to seek out a reasonable middle ground on the issues. Of course, Eisenhower's years as President had given him an appreciation of national politics which no other general could have, and Ike's latter-day approach to military problems was always tempered by these considerations. Almost as often as not, this put him on the side of the civilians as opposed to the military, a result which was particularly heartening to Johnson.

"I tried for one whole year to do in Vietnam what Kennedy did in Laos, to get some kind of an agreement so we wouldn't have to go in there," Johnson once said. I recall the sadness with which Bill Moyers, reflecting the President's views, surveyed the future when the dark hand of the war unmistakably gripped the Administration and the Great Society was being restrained. Johnson had begun to feel that he was to play much the same role in history as Harry Truman, a man who had hoped that his country after four years of war could turn its energies inward but who found that much of his leadership had to be given to the threat of war and to actual war. Johnson had wanted to emulate the New Deal, to build up and not blow up. Thus, reluctantly, almost angrily, he turned in 1966 to being a War President.

Even the most casual observer of Johnson could detect the difference in enthusiasm. Talking about the war was plainly a chore, designed to present a point or answer a critic, carried through competently but with no great spirit. His dissertations often were accompanied by long readings from the reports of his generals and ambassadors, done because in those matters Johnson just did not have the same understanding or motivation as in domestic affairs.

When Johnson began to talk about controlling rivers to produce power and water, he became more animated, he discarded notes, his arguments became more convincing. That subject he knew and loved. Even after attaining the Presidency, Johnson told visitors that nothing had gratified him as a Congressman more than development of the Lower Colorado River. Sometimes when Johnson finished one of his tours of his Boyhood Home in Johnson City he would go up to the Pedernales Electric Coop., just a block away, there to gaze wistfully at that handsome limestone building with the plaque on the wall which said that the Coop., once the biggest in the United States, was a product of the "faith, ability and foresight of Lyndon Baines Johnson, President of the United States of America, while Congressman from the Tenth District, 1938." It was, too.

When he first visited the Mekong Valley as Vice President, he envisioned power lines and orderly farm fields. He stood in Korea below Seoul on the hill named Lyndon B. Johnson and dreamed the same way. In his office, at the end of a long, tiring discussion about the fighting in Vietnam, Johnson's aides saw light come into his eyes as he began to talk about the success of the new rice seed in India and how it meant more prosperity and security for all of Asia. After his Honolulu meeting with South Vietnam's Premier Ky, Johnson dispatched agriculture and economic experts to South Vietnam with far more joy than he did more troops. He asked for reports on improving the hog marketing, on dampening inflation, curtailing the black market, diversifying small farms and all the other topics that he knew about. He may never have been more ecstatic over Vietnam than when he made his Johns Hopkins speech in April of 1965 and pledged a billion-dollar scheme for the development of Southeast Asia. It rang of New Deal oratory, referring to the Mekong River development as if it were the Tennessee Valley. His search for someone to head the new Asian Development Bank was one of those Johnson spectaculars into which he poured all his energy and skill. He remained unsatisfied until, on the very day he gave his speech, one of his staff members finally came up with the name of the urbane New York financier Eugene Black. This suggestion drew instant approval from LBJ. There was then no rest until Black had been tracked down by telephone at lunch in New York and pressured to take the job, then fly to Washington for the announcement.

Johnson's international enthusiasm followed the lines laid down by the economist Barbara Ward. Her messianic materialism was a sort of global New Deal. "The Christian God who bade his followers feed the hungry and heal the sick and took his parables from the homely round of daily work gave material things his benediction," she wrote. The President kept a copy of her book *The Rich Nations and the Poor Nations* beside his bed.

If there was a strain of unbending sincerity in Johnson, it was his inner zeal to ease some of the misery of this life for others.

He talked often when he was President about seeing the people of his area "age before their time" from grinding work and bitter disappointment. He told a story of going to his sobbing mother as she numbly pumped water one midnight when he was four years old and his father was gone. He put his arms around her legs and told her not to worry, he would take care of her. From the White House Johnson still flew to visit the old family friends, and when he found them as invalids in cramped rooms, burdens to young families, he came back and talked with new energy about the need for nursing homes and for medical help for the old. And all of this was so far from the talk of war, and the planning for war and the destruction left by war, that perhaps Johnson could be excused for not ever really accepting the counsel of some that he would have to abandon his majestic ideas for American society if he was to fulfill the mission he had undertaken in Vietnam. There was no pleasure in waging war. There was only the grim, plodding business of trying to figure out best how to uphold the national honor with the least cost and in the shortest time. And the answer just was not very pleasant, and it grew more difficult as time went on.

Against this Populist current of compassion ran another—the simple manly compulsion to act with courage. In Johnson's case, however, this instinct was magnified by Texas legend and his own sense of exaggeration. A part of it was the "Alamo syndrome" mentioned earlier. If there was anything that Johnson feared during his White House residence, it was that the historians might say he was not a brave leader. He reduced the history that he lived each hour to the most personal terms because of this worry. "I'm not going down in history as the man responsible for another Castro," he said to one aide after he had sent the Marines to the Dominican Republic. Only hours after he became Chief Executive and the grieving Ambassador Henry Cabot Lodge dragged himself to the new President's office to warn that some terribly important decisions had to be made very soon on Vietnam, Johnson blurted, "I'm not going to go down in history as the first American President who lost a war." Once when he explained his Vietnam commitment he was right back with the

early Texans. "Just like the Alamo," he said, "somebody damn well needed to go to their aid. Well, by God,
I'm going to Vietnam's aid." This was worrisome to
many who understood this streak in Johnson's make-up.
It was too simplistic for this age, the theory went. There
was the vague uneasiness that his concern for legend
prevented him from prodding as energetically and as
skillfully as possible for a diplomatic solution to Vietnam which might be murky and just not very spectacular. The "Matt Dillon" facet of Johnson's character
perhaps was not that important, but it was Johnson
himself who constantly reminded people of it. Back in
1960 he had personally told Kennedy's Press Secretary,
Pierre Salinger, to sell the Johnson image as one of "a
big, tall, tough Texan." In the troublesome summer of
1961, as Vice President, he met and reviewed the convoy
which had gone across East Germany to test the Rus-
sians, and afterward he passed out autographed pictures
of the stern visages of himself and Konrad Adenauer
with the proud comment, "Look at those strong faces."
He had not talked much about the Silver Star which he
won in the South Pacific. But as the war progressed and
courage became one of the necessary political staples,
Johnson could tell a rather gripping story about "that
Japanese ace" who was machine-gunning the bomber
on which he rode as an observer. Johnson's feeling
about individual men was often reduced to simple
terms of courage and endurance. When the great chorus
was raised against Dean Rusk in 1965 and some like
historian Arthur Schlesinger were suggesting that Rusk

should resign, Johnson said admiringly of his Buddha-like Secretary of State, "He takes all they can give and is stronger than ever." Johnson's assessment of one of his closest friends, business partners and Texas neighbors, Judge A. W. Moursund, read like a Hollywood scenario: the Judge could survey a line, break a horse, skin a deer, best big-city attorneys in the courtroom and "whup" anybody within sight. There was a lot of simple respect for the old-fashioned hero left in Lyndon Johnson, and it profoundly affected his decisions about Vietnam. To what extent no one could measure, since it all got mixed up in the chambers of his mind conditioned by his years of existence in the legislative Byzantium. When he could, he took long agony to arrive at a decision, but once there, he lifted a battle standard of the simple virtues of courage and righteousness. In the fall of 1967, when he found he lived in a city that no longer believed in him and the country was on the brink of political desertion, he turned to history for companionship and solace.

He called the roll to visitors—Washington at Valley Forge; Madison during the war of 1812; Abraham Lincoln in the Civil War; Woodrow Wilson and the "small band of wilful men"; Franklin Roosevelt and Harry Truman. Even John Kennedy joined this elite because Johnson recalled an issue of *Time* which was dated November 22, 1963, and Kennedy's fortunes had been mighty low. There was almost a sense of pride in Johnson's loneliness; never quite expressed by the President but hinted at was the feeling that, like these others, he had been chosen by history to suffer indignities from the short-sighted, but then to be vindicated and raised to the lofty pedestal reserved for the strong. There was perhaps more truth to this than a lot of critics cared to admit. The more lonely a President's course, the greater the impact of his results. And, generally speaking, the crisis Presidents have been more right than the loud critics.

His patriotism was fundamental. Once on a platform he jabbed a finger toward the U.S. flag and cried, "Where American citizens go, that flag goes with them to protect them. . . . As a little boy I learned a declamation that I had to say in grade school. I don't remember all of it, but a little of it is appropriate here this afternoon. It went something like this: 'I have seen the glory of art and architecture. I have seen the sunrise on Mount Blanc, but the most beautiful vision that these eyes have beheld was the flag of my country in a foreign land.'"

Underlying all of this was Johnson's view of history. That view went neither very far backward (except when he summoned the other Presidents to his side) nor very far forward. It was the living, breathing experience that he himself had had in national and international affairs. Either as counselor or legislator or Vice President or President, Johnson had taken some part in every important action of this country in thirty years. No other living man had such a stockpile of contemporary experience. No leader—Wilson or De Gaulle or Kosygin—had been privileged to examine such a broad horizon of statecraft. Johnson lunched with Roosevelt as he ended the New Deal and turned to running the war. He was Speaker Rayburn's ally in the fateful battle to extend the draft just two months before Pearl Harbor. Johnson can recall in intense detail the drama of that day which began in Rayburn's apartment at breakfast when defeat appeared certain and ended on the floor of the House when Rayburn, ignoring the last-minute entry of two Congressmen, smashed his gavel down and pronounced the draft extension passed—by one vote. Johnson worried about our rapid demobilization after the war, watched Truman command the Berlin Airlift and then fight the Korean War. He championed aid to Greece and Turkey and then the Marshall Plan. He studied Truman's seizure of the railroads and the steel mills. As the Senate Leader, he was always consulted by Eisenhower before any major domestic or international move. Johnson saw and met the important visitors who came to this country, including Nikita Khrushchev at the time he flew to the United Nations in 1960. Johnson probed deep into the nation's preparedness in the late 1950's and he was a major force behind our space effort. He watched John Kennedy's leadership from its center. He was informed on the events leading up to the overthrow and murder of South Vietnam's Ngo Dinh Diem. He was fully briefed on the Bay of Pigs and then the Cuban missile crisis. And, of course, his report as Vice President from Vietnam was among the first of many that came to Kennedy warning him of the struggle developing there.

Because he was so heavily involved in real events from such an early age, Johnson never became a scholar. His sense of history was one-generational. He picked up fragments about Presidents and statesmen when he needed them or when he ran across them in his conversations with others. But he rarely read books, and when he did, it was not likely that he went from cover to cover, but fished around for useful items that met his immediate demands. Having done a *Life* article about Kennedy's ravenous appetite for books and how he read at 1,200 words a minute, I thought of doing the same sort of review of Johnson's reading. My first stop at George Reedy's office brought the testimony that Johnson was an avid reader of history and government. The only book that George could think of, however, which had gotten the President's recent attention was Barbara Ward's *The Rich Nations and the Poor Nations*. I pursued my inquiry to Bill Moyers, who said that Johnson read books when he had time. Which ones? Moyers thought, then jubilantly said that the President had particularly liked Barbara Ward's *The Rich Nations and the Poor Nations*. The next stop was Jack Valenti, who unabashedly rated Johnson as a rapid and wide-ranging book consumer. Jack hesitated a bit when asked for titles. Then his face lighted up: Barbara Ward's *The Rich Nations and the Poor Nations*. Once when Johnson was talking to his legislative leaders about Vietnam, he ended the session by picking up a copy of Bruce Catton's *Never Call Retreat* and reading a portion on the anguish of Lincoln during the dark months of the Civil War. Johnson explained that he had been reading the book the other night and come across the passage. Actually, Bobby Kennedy had found the relevant sentences and that very day had sent the book to Johnson with a sympathetic notation.

Only rarely was Johnson interested in things that came before his time, as Eric Goldman learned. But events which he had witnessed got his thorough and singular attention. He was in an unusual manner a student of others' errors. He was totally fascinated by what went wrong, why people had failed, what weaknesses they manifested. On the Hill he had been a virtual encyclopedia of the fallibility of his fellow legislators. The knowledge gave him power. He knew how to get to a man, how to capitalize on his soft spots. In a sense, the course of his Presidency was set by the adjustments which he made to avoid the pitfalls encountered by the men of power whom he had known. He used that measure in all matters. Assaulting industrialists had only made Franklin Roosevelt's life more difficult. Johnson did not see the sense in such an attack, nor in that of Kennedy on the big steel men whom JFK labeled "SOB's." The most cogent lessons to Johnson, though, were those in national security. They began with Neville Chamberlain's appeasement of Hitler, they were brought home by the United States debates over fortifying Guam, Lend-Lease for the allies, and the draft. The lessons went on with the Berlin Blockade and our lack of preparedness for Korea. There was the missile-gap debate and then the space lag. Johnson looked closely at the trouble in Laos, and that was followed by the Bay of Pigs, and then Vietnam was the issue, only to be interrupted by the Cuban crisis, and then Johnson was President and in rapid sequence faced some minor crises like the Cuban cut-off of water to our naval base in Guantánamo, the riots in Panama, and the Dominican Republic uprising. Vietnam rose again and smothered everything else. The central theme which Johnson found running through this span of history was that when the United States weakened its defense structure or ignored its world responsibilities or when its leaders hesitated or vacillated, rarely did we escape trouble and when it came the trouble was usually worse than it would have been earlier. "We're not going to have any men with any umbrellas," Johnson said, applying the 1938 image to the Vietnam war.

Our involvement in the Vietnam war has been chronicled many times in many places. From Eisenhower through Kennedy, the momentum of our good intentions carried us into a bog that nobody seemed to want to enter but nobody knew how to avoid. Johnson's reaction to the attacks on the destroyer *Maddox* in the Gulf of Tonkin in August of 1964 was instant and firm. At least two of the enemy gunboats were sunk and the boat pens along the coast of North Vietnam were attacked by Navy carrier planes. And yet a few weeks later, in the campaign, the President was declaring, "We are not about to send American boys nine or ten thousand miles away from home to do what Asian boys ought to be doing to protect themselves."

Privately he was saying, "If one little ole general in shirt sleeves can take Saigon, think about two hundred million Chinese coming down those trails. No sir, I don't want to fight them." He was equally vehement about Barry Goldwater and his belligerent talk in the campaign. "We can't let Goldwater and Red China both get the bomb at the same time. Then the shit would really hit the fan."

A few days before the election, when twenty-six planes were destroyed in attacks at Danang and Chulai, Ambassador Maxwell Taylor recommended a retaliatory air attack against North Vietnam. But it was too close then to the balloting, and a country swept up in the excitement of the Presidential run-off hardly noted that Johnson did nothing. In early February of 1965, when Air Force barracks at Pleiku were attacked with mortars and hand grenades and eight Americans killed, there was no hesitation. United States bombers struck North Vietnam, and perhaps from that time on the total involvement of Lyndon Johnson, and the U.S., in that far-off war was inevitable. Johnson, who had been preoccupied with learning about the Presidency and getting elected in his own right, began to learn more about the war he was waging, and in the spring and early summer of 1965 it was apparent he was on the brink of disaster. The war was very close to being lost. North Vietnamese regulars were slipping down the Ho Chi Minh trail along the eastern border of Laos. The Viet Cong were fighting in main-force units, the final phase of their very carefully calibrated plans to take over South Vietnam.

There were two basic options open to the President. He could get out of Vietnam or he could send a major force of combat troops to take the offensive—to fight toward some kind of victory, even though not clearly defined. Actually, there was only one option, given the state of Lyndon Johnson's mind and, indeed, of the national mentality. The United States did not quit and run. Thus it was almost inevitable from May and June on that we would have a "Korean-size" commitment before long in Vietnam. Johnson was gloomy over the prospects not only because of his campaign promises to stay out but because of the contemplation of years of killing. He was somewhat disillusioned at this time in the advice he was getting. He confided to friends that he could not be certain of the facts and the assessments which his generals were sending him. He used to pull cables from his pockets and read the optimistic statistics about enemy killed and desertion rates. It had dawned on him, as the situation worsened, that they were meaningless. It was plain to almost anyone who could read the newspapers that the 75,000 men we had were not enough to contend with the storm which the Viet Cong was then creating. Talking to a group of foreign correspondents whom columnist Max Freedman had assembled in early July, Johnson made it clear that as many men as needed would be sent to Vietnam. He was in a tough frame of mind, suggesting that the United States would "fight to its last soldier" if necessary. Johnson's jaw was set.

The President was further disheartened by the lack of response from Hanoi. In a curious way, he was much like John Kennedy when the latter met Khrushchev in Vienna. Kennedy expected the Russian to be a man of some reason. But when they discussed the millions of casualties which would result from nuclear war and Khrushchev seemed indifferent to such annihilation, Kennedy was shaken. Ho Chi Minh's silence in Hanoi was unfathomable to Johnson, who had often said that he had never known a man with whom he could not find some area of understanding if the two could sit down and talk face to face. "Old Man Ho," as Johnson called him, apparently had never come under the spell of the Prophet Isaiah. Besides, he was ten thousand miles away and Johnson was not used to working at such distances.

"What people don't seem to realize is that the Viet Cong believe they are winning," Johnson told his guests. The fact was, of course, that the Viet Cong *were* winning. "Why should they negotiate for a slice of bread if they are convinced they can win the whole loaf?" LBJ asked his experts. Johnson watched the polls closely during those weeks. He was profoundly interested in finding out how well the folks felt he was running the war. His concern was even more for the future. As he realized that more men would have to be committed to the fighting, he worried about the impact of the casualties on the national state of mind. Of course, he considered the political impact on his Presidency, but he was even more concerned about the effect on the will of the people to wage war.

Realizing the importance of the commitment he was about to make, the President departed from his customary secrecy and began to condition the nation for war on a major scale. At a press conference in mid-July he announced that McNamara and Lodge would leave the next evening for Saigon on a fact-finding mission. "When they return next week," he said, "we will give careful consideration to their recommendations as well as those of Ambassador Taylor and General Westmoreland. We will do what is necessary. . . . Increased aggression from the North may require an increased American response on the ground in South Vietnam." Johnson paused for a few seconds as he squinted into the klieg lights above the television cameras. "So it is quite possible that new and serious decisions will be necessary in the near future. Any substantial increase in the present level of our efforts to turn back the aggressors in South Vietnam will require steps to insure that our reserves of men and equipment of the United States remain entirely adequate for any and all emergencies." In the last statement there was the hint that Johnson was considering calling up the reserves. And at that time he was.

Johnson was at last leaving that "improbable world" of his own creation which he had talked about in his 1964 campaign. The realities of international politics were weighing in on him, as they inevitably had to. The grand predictions of a short war, the hopeful statistics of his generals, his own vast dreams for building that perfect society all began to give way to the very real world. Johnson entered it talking—talking to all those around him and to his nation. It was his catharsis, his thought process. Meeting with his National Security Council, he looked ahead and what he saw was not pleasant, and he told one of his Texas jokes to illustrate his state of mind. "That reminds me of two Indians," he said. "The first invited the second home to dinner. 'What are you having?' asked the second. 'Crow,' said the first. 'Crow—that's not fit to eat, is it?' complained the second. 'Better'n owl,' replied the first." So Johnson was eating crow, but maybe it was better than something else.

As McNamara and Lodge flew toward Saigon, Johnson went late one afternoon to the Rose Garden to address one of his favorite groups, the National Electric Cooperative Association. He talked wistfully of the things that he liked. "Of all the work that I have been privileged to do in my public career, nothing has been more gratifying to me than my association with the rural electrification program. By many measurements that program stands today as one of the most successful enterprises ever undertaken anywhere, at any time, by anyone." For a moment he found a parallel. "I never go home for a weekend and look over a series of six beautiful lakes but what I remember when I was almost burned at the stake. . . . Now, you have to stand up to that kind of heat while you are doing this kind of planning, and I think that you must also, as I know you are, turn your attention to horizons that are beyond your country, and your state, and your nation, because you are living in a pretty big world." Rather sadly Johnson found himself facing that same bleak view across the Pacific. "We have commitments and we intend to keep them. . . . And our national honor is at stake in Southeast Asia and we are going to protect it, and you just might as well be prepared for it, and we can do it better if we are united." Not before, nor really since, has Johnson been more open and more eloquent in a fundamental way than he was that day only a week before he gave the final orders that started hundreds of thousands of American men toward Vietnam. The late sun slanted across the Rose Garden in full summer bloom. Johnson was standing with leather-faced men from farms and ranches across the country. His mind was made up about Vietnam, although he would spend a week in intensive review trying to see if there was some other way to go. There was no other way, however, and he understood that when he spoke. "We do not expect the road to be smooth, and you just be sure it is not going to be short. But we do intend that the end result shall be a better world where men of all lands and all colors and all cultures can enjoy in their lifetime something of the advances that we have known in our lifetime. . . . We love peace. . . . We hate war. . . . Now there are going to be some dark days, and there are going to be some times when we may call on you for some help, and I don't think you will be found wanting."

Johnson's great week of review began on July 21 and

it ended at noon on July 28, when he went on television to inform the country of his decision. The deliberations were held in the Cabinet Room, an ominous chamber where the cold light of a blue-white neon grid gives a somber burnish to the dark mahogany of the eight-sided table where the course of civilization is debated. The preparations were formalized as never before, with two dozen of the top Administration men attending, their faces reflecting, like those of James Monroe, Daniel Webster and Andrew Jackson who stared from the walls, the very serious business of leading a country. Every morning Johnson came in and pulled up his huge black leather chair with the tiny brass plate on the back: THE PRESIDENT. He hunched forward on his elbows, and the parade of witnesses that lasted through the day began. This was a singular command post. Below the lip of the table was a white button labeled: JUANITA—the buzzer to Juanita Roberts, LBJ's personal secretary. A white telephone hung at knee height. Before him on the table were a worn green blotter, a small note pad, a yellow legal tablet and two Venus Forum Number One pencils, freshly sharpened. These were the only tools. Beyond the windows at the President's back was the Rose Garden. The thermostat inside was set at 66 degrees so that Johnson would not grow uncomfortable from the human heat. On the mantel above the fireplace the old clock from the former Presidential yacht, the *Williamsburg*, ticked off the more than twenty-five hours of meetings that were held. They must have been intense meetings because when they were over there were no doodles left on the pads in front of Johnson. He had been too absorbed to scribble.

In many ways Johnson had created an educational forum. He wanted the country to prepare for what was coming and he wanted the enemy to know that he was going further in, not getting out. At the same time he wanted to quiet mounting complaints about his secret and erratic methods of making decisions.

The seven days of deliberation in July were useful and, perhaps, even necessary in that they helped focus the Administration's thinking and won a broad consensus within the government for Johnson's decision. But they changed nothing about Johnson's decision process. His mind had reached its conclusion long before. What he sought was a deep factual underpinning for the war he was to wage.

The nature of that war was a torment. At first LBJ was not fully aware of the difference between fighting for territory, as in other wars, and fighting this war, which was a war to prove our determination to the enemy in hopes he might call it all off and at the same time to win the hearts and minds of those we were fighting for. Victory was a vague concept allowing us to withdraw our troops without losing face and at the same guaranteeing South Vietnam the right to self-determination even if its choice was Ho Chi Minh's reign. Johnson roamed the back corridors of the White House in those agonizing days, trying to sort out political objectives from military objectives, making certain that he fixed in his mind the priorities. To those to whom he talked he would say, "It used to be a lot simpler. Franklin Roosevelt's order to Eisenhower was 'Seek out the German army and destroy it.'" Then Johnson would point out how such instructions in this murky war were not only undesirable but impossible. In the course of Johnson's great forum his strategists came up with five alternatives that formed the basis of discussion.

The first: The United States could go all the way in waging the war, destroying North Vietnam and anything else in the path of our horrendous machine. This alternative was scarcely considered.

The second: We could pull out. That, too, was rejected from the start.

The third: We could continue to do what we were doing. Since all the experts testified that we were then losing the war, this alternative was discarded.

The fourth: The United States could increase its commitment, give the commanders what they needed to fight an effective but limited war, and rally the home front to meet the new challenge by declaring a national emergency, calling up some reserve units and having Johnson go before Congress with a special request for funds.

The fifth: The fourth alternative minus all the theatrics. No bands playing, no reserve call-up if possible, no national emergency or special appearance before Congress.

Option four occupied the first few days of debate. Dean Rusk favored some form of national involvement, and so did other politically oriented men around the

table. In a sense, it was the summer of 1961 all over
again, when Kennedy faced the crunch in Berlin and
decided to call up some reserve units and ask Congress
for a special appropriation. To White House aides,
option four became "fire in the sky" and Johnson worried it through several sessions of his assemblage.

LBJ was the interrogator. At one such session he
asked over one hundred questions, by the count kept
meticulously by Bill Moyers. The log of those days was
typically Johnson. He tried some of his schoolteacher's
gimmicks. He asked the military experts to evaluate the
political recommendations and then, in turn, asked the
political men to analyze the military suggestions. This
was a worthless process, but Johnson was constantly
doing it because he felt it looked good in the news
stories. There was a lot of Johnson's patriotic hyperbole
thrown in. That, too, was obviously offered for public
consumption. But, basically, Johnson was sincere, and
his anxiety prompted his long questioning. The facts,
unfortunately, all bore out the President's earlier contention that he had to go into South Vietnam and fight.
This was the burden of the McNamara-Lodge report.
Johnson at first sought for the "feel of the situation."
He asked detailed questions about the Viet Cong sol-
diers themselves. What were they like? How was their
morale? What kind of information did we get from the
captured Viet Cong? He explored the casualty rates and
was warned that they would rise sharply if we increased
our forces and sought out the enemy. "The forty-eight
men we lost last week already are a worry to me,"

Johnson sighed. He poured over the detailed maps showing all the Viet Cong strongholds and he studied for many long minutes the photographs of the bridges and highways which the VC had destroyed.

Johnson sought out old friends such as Everett Dirksen. What might Dirksen do if faced with the problem? Johnson asked. The Minority Leader knew his place and he also was too politically wise to plunge into that thicket. "This is a military matter," said Dirksen. "I am not equipped to make such a decision. You, sir, are the Commander-in-Chief. You, sir, have to decide." Johnson smiled. He knew that answer all too well.

He wanted full answers from his men. If one course of action was to be followed, then what would be likely to result? The weaknesses of option four began to appear under the repeated questions. There was no guarantee that the Defense Department could make effective use of any reserves. They might just mark time for a few weeks while their equipment was being marshaled and the plans for deployment worked out. Johnson disliked that idea. The diplomatic intelligence suggested that if too much fuss was made about the increased effort in the war, both Russia and Red China might find it necessary to match our new input. McNamara came up with figures to show that the reserves would not be needed for their manpower—the Defense Department could handle the new troop requirements if a reasonable build-up was undertaken. While the Johnson council of war met, there was considerable flag-waving on the outside, most military partisans suggesting that the country be put on a war footing of one degree or another. Around the White House this fixation was called "the Army-Navy Club syndrome."

In these days Johnson began to repeat to his staff and those who came to see him in the Oval Office his view of history, repeating many times the trials of Roosevelt and Truman and recounting John Kennedy's ordeal with the Cuban missiles. "The road to peace is not through weakness," he told those with him. "Appeasement would be disaster." It was then that Johnson devised his "two wars to win" idiom, claiming that McNamara was to handle the shooting war and Rusk the diplomatic war. "McNamara will get us in," he said, "and Rusk will get us out."

That Johnson was skeptical of "fire in the sky" from almost the first day of his week's review was known by a few intimates. To a staff member he confided, "I've got grave doubts. . . . I don't want to make any decisions until I have gone over this whole thing. . . . I don't want a Third World War. . . . I want more discussion and debate. Tell Bundy to schedule these meetings right around the clock if it is necessary." He even grew a little testy in his interrogations. "What do you mean, 'control the area'?" asked LBJ about one of those all-purpose generalizations that crop up in such discussions. "How do the villagers feel? . . . What do they say, what do they do? . . . You fellows say that the bombing is effective. What does that mean? Let's see the figures." When one general talked about the South Vietnamese army being "fine," Johnson was downright doubtful.

"How do we know? . . . How is their morale? . . . How many deserted last month?" Brooding still about plunging the entire country into the war, the President declared, "I think that more wars are started through conveying the wrong intentions than through any other way."

When the deliberations would begin to look back for who was to blame for our presence there, Johnson wisely cut off the debate. "We may have made mistakes," he said, "and we may not have made mistakes. But that is not my problem. My problem is what to do tomorrow."

On Friday afternoon, option four lost out. Johnson looked around at his men. "I've got just a little weak spot in my stomach," he said, putting his hand to his ample middle. "The answer is 'No.' I'm going up to Camp David." Long hours in the Catoctin Mountains cleared his mind. He came back Monday reasonably convinced, as he was to tell it later, that he could meet Westmoreland's requests "without provoking the Soviet Union, the Chinese, the French or anyone else beyond a permissible level."

There was another reason why the President decided that his response should be low-key. While he was at Camp David the news had broken that one of our F4C's had been downed over Hanoi by a Russian-supplied surface-to-air missile (SAM). When McNamara first phoned the report to Camp David there was some doubt. But evidence that trickled in all day Monday confirmed the stark facts. This was yet another dimension to the war. Monday night Johnson called his closest advisers to a highly secret two-hour meeting to debate the response to the loss of the plane. Johnson felt that by acting with firmness and promptness in this incident he would deliver part of the message to the enemy which he had been considering in the discussions of the preceding days. The others around the Cabinet table were in agreement and Johnson heard each man speak. He turned to General Wheeler. "How long will it take to knock the missiles out after I give the order?" he asked. Wheeler estimated "about six or seven hours." Johnson thought a moment. "Is there any other comment?" he asked, sweeping his eyes around the room. Nobody spoke. For a few silent seconds the room seemed cold and hard in the neon glare. The President swung his chair around and looked at McNamara. "Okay," he said, "take 'em out."

That decision apparently resolved LBJ's other doubts. Tuesday, after Navy planes had blasted the missile sites, he declared that he would follow option five in giving Westmoreland the troops he wanted, but as quietly as possible.

On Tuesday night Johnson summoned the legislative leaders, not so much for consultation as to tell them of his decision. As expected, Ev Dirksen was solidly in the President's corner. Ev approved of the muted marshaling of the forces. "I remember," he told Johnson, "World War I when Teddy Roosevelt wanted to raise a brigade and go to Europe to fight. President Woodrow Wilson stopped that with one sentence: 'The business at hand is undramatic.' " Johnson looked appreciatively at his old friend across the table. "That's exactly the way I feel about it, Everett," he said. "The fewer theatrics the better." Johnson did rather an effective job in minimizing partisan politics that evening. One aide remembers that as the leaders' meeting broke up, the President had a last thought and suddenly lifted his hands for silence. "One more thing," he said. "I didn't call you down here as Republicans and Democrats. Those aren't Republican or Democratic boys over there fighting. Those are American boys and this is an American war." What might have been embarrassingly corny in another context somehow on that somber night hit the right chord. The two dozen men turned and cheered.

Harmony had not been complete that night, however. Johnson's own party leader in the Senate, Mike Mansfield, had pulled a three-page statement from his pocket and read it in full. It was familiar Mansfield doctrine, a dissent to sending more troops, continued objection to the bombing of the north, disenchantment, really, with our whole Vietnam policy. And yet Mansfield was ever the loyal trooper despite his personal misgivings. When he had finished reading his statement, he went on. "I want you to know, Mr. President, when you make your decision I am going to support it. I am going to support it on the Senate floor, I'm going to support it as Majority Leader, I'm going to support it as a Senator from Montana."

It was near midnight when the President finally

233

planned for the next day. He had to inform the nation. He deliberately chose a press conference at midday when the TV audience would be reduced.

Already it had been decided that his statement would follow pretty closely some things the President had said earlier when talking with McNamara and Rusk. He had been in one of his thoughtful moods, and even though his language was overdone, his message had come through. "All my life I've wanted to build for the American people," he told these men. "And I want to resolve this thing honorably, so that I can carry out these things that I've wanted to do. . . . When I was a young man, water was life itself. . . . People were very poor. . . . We have worked and struggled to get these things, and every time we have gotten near the culmination of our dreams, the war bells have rung. If we have to fight, I'll do that. But I don't want you to forget that those things are what people want. . . . I don't want to be known as a War President."

Finally, on Tuesday night, there was not much more for the President to say or do. Richard Goodwin headed for his typewriter to write a "war speech that sounds like a peace speech." Goodwin wrote all night, finishing at five a.m. Copies were sped by White House limousine to the homes of Rusk and McNamara, and, of course, one was taken to the door of the slumbering President.

The press conference that day at which Johnson would announce his decision to send 50,000 more troops, forerunners of many more (though he would not say that publicly then), was one of those special

Johnson concoctions. Not only did he explain his Vietnam decision but he announced the appointment of attorney Abe Fortas as a Supreme Court Justice and NBC's John Chancellor as the new head of the Voice of America. He did not want all the headlines to go to the war.

The East Room was a nightmare of paraphernalia because of Johnson's special demands. There were huge lighting devices, backdrops, a special umbrella reflector over LBJ's head and a giant machine, known as the "people eater," into which Johnson talked when he wanted to read from a teleprompter without appearing to do so. It all would have seemed ludicrous, except for the somber message.

Johnson read a letter from a Midwestern soldier's mother asking why our country was at war. "Why must young Americans, born into a land exultant with hope and with golden promise, toil and suffer and sometimes die in such a remote and distant place? We have learned at a terrible and brutal cost that retreat does not bring safety and weakness does not bring peace." Johnson explained that most Asian nations could not withstand the ambition of Asian communists. "Our power, therefore, is a very vital shield. If we are driven from the field in Vietnam, then no nation can ever again have the same confidence in American promises or in American protection. . . . We did not choose to be the guardians at the gate, but there is no one else." The President ran through the troop statistics—the increase from 75,000 to 125,000, the draft hike from 17,000 per month to 35,000, his decision not to call the reserves. He told of his hopes to build rather than to destroy. "But I also know, as a realistic public servant," Johnson declared, "that as long as there are men who hate and destroy, we must have the courage to resist, or we will see it all, all that we have built, all that we hope to build, all of our dreams for freedom—all—all—will be swept away on the flood of conquest. So, too, this shall not happen. . . . We shall stand in Vietnam."

There was no turning back from then on. The 50,000 troops swelled to 100,000, and then the grand total rose to 525,000, the cost to $30 billion a year, and yet none of this, in terms of national resources, was a very major problem. The great trouble was in the minds of the people. And, naturally, the question arose whether Johnson had erred by not in some manner having involved the American public in the war. He had always considered the call-up of reserves by John Kennedy in the summer of 1961 to be one of Kennedy's major policy blunders, pointing to the fact that some of the units did not have weapons or other equipment and simply sat around ineffectually until their time expired. But Johnson failed utterly to grasp the larger significance of how that move had mobilized United States opinion behind Kennedy and had signaled the Soviet Union as clearly as anything that we did not intend to abandon Berlin. In his Vietnam decision Johnson reverted to his old form, trying not to commit himself as either hawk or dove, declaring his intent to win the war (if the other side did not negotiate before that) but at the same time

declaring that the nation would scarcely have to incon-
venience itself while fighting this war ten thousand
miles off. Guns and butter may have been the most
faulty equation which Johnson ever devised in his political years.

Once Johnson had made his Vietnam decision, he
exploded. It was as if a great store of energy had been
released. Doubling the war effort, appointing Fortas to
the Supreme Court and Chancellor to the VOA had
only whetted his appetite. He swore in Arthur Goldberg
as Ambassador to the United Nations, nominated John
Gardner to be his Secretary of Health, Education and
Welfare. He signed bills that poured from Congress,
such as the cautionary-labeling act for cigarettes. He
limousined to the Pentagon to pay tribute to their cost-
cutting and there joked about out-bowling McNamara
at Camp David. He escorted house guests on personal-
ized tours of the mansion, conferred with Eugene Black
about the Asian Development Bank ("My, he's a smart
man. I learn more in thirty minutes from him than I
learned in all my economics courses.") He flew all fifty
governors in from Minneapolis for a special briefing on
Vietnam, dashed off to Independence, Missouri, to sign
the Medicare bill in the presence of Harry Truman. He
talked with a task force from the AMA about the imple-
menting of Medicare and he signed papers for a $35-
million loan to the Central American Development
Bank. Johnson gabbed with lady reporters over coffee
about the great support he received from wives and
mothers in his Vietnam decision. It was Johnson's sin-

gular manner of showing that he was proud of what he had decided and that he was still the man in charge, a man of legendary energy.

He even found time, when all the dust had settled, to talk quietly for an hour about his private feelings concerning the course he had set in Vietnam. "Russia doesn't want war, China doesn't want to get into a war and you know damned well that we don't want to get into the big war. We can do this thing without bluster, without throwing our weight around. And we can do it, still making clear that you must win." Some heavy weight was off the President's shoulders as he sat in his small study just down the hall from the Oval Office. It had gone as he had wanted it to. "This government just played like a great big piano, without hitting a sour note," he said, and for a few seconds he raised his big hands and was playing an imaginary keyboard in the air. He had devised by then his prizefighter analogy that soon would be standard fare whenever he met with those who wanted to know his approach to Vietnam. "I told McNamara that he was my right-hand punch. I told him to take the power of this country and with it keep our word and keep our honor and our treaty and protect the lives of our boys to the maximum extent possible [Johnson raised his right fist]. I told Rusk and Goldberg that they're my left-hand punch [he cocked his left and punched the imaginary target] and to try to get us out."

Despite the new effort in Vietnam, he would hardly tolerate the thought of backing away from any part of his Great Society programs. Guns and butter to the end. "You'll always have people who live up on a high hill and want to keep other people down; who are willing to go along with poverty, misery, illiteracy, ill health. I believe this country needs all the brains and all the healthy bodies it can get. I don't intend to let this war stop that."

But war is a monster and even a war that is only four percent of the gross national product stops a lot. Johnson's 1968 program held a desperately thin domestic line. When North Korea seized the spy ship *Pueblo* in early 1968, he had to call up air reserves to meet the new challenge. And the communist offensive against the cities made even more troops seem inevitable. The monster grew.

Despite the periodic claims by foreign diplomats and domestic doves that Hanoi was ready to negotiate, there was no firm word that the enemy was really interested in stopping the fighting. Johnson tried two bombing pauses and got nothing. His peace offensives in which he dispatched diplomats around the world got no sincere nibbles. He refined his Johns Hopkins position and told Hanoi that he would stop the bombing of North Vietnam and be ready to sit down if they would only indicate that they would not take advantage of the pause and increase their build-up. He would accept normal supply and infiltration while talks went on. To show his good faith, he drew rings around Hanoi and Haiphong and twice restricted bombing in those areas, and he sent precise word to the enemy each time. He spelled out his offer publicly in a speech in San Antonio when the private contacts failed to produce a signal. There was no response. "They can't ever be accused of being hypocrites," Johnson said bitterly. "They've given the same answer from the start. It is just like the answer that Travis gave at the Alamo when they asked if he would surrender. A cannon shot."

A determined Johnson hunkered down. "I read the papers," he once mused. "Burdett or Schoenbrun or one of those correspondents has got the word. I come to the office next morning thinking that Ho has got to be on the line. But he isn't, and we can't fool ourselves about it. It's like an old cowboy used to say, 'There's no use being poor and stupid all your life when you can buy a pint of whiskey and be rich and smart in an hour.' We can't do that."

REFLECTION

You could stand on this Tuesday afternoon in February of 1967 and look out over the faces in the East Room of the White House and suddenly understand that Franklin Roosevelt still owned Washington. His ideas prevailed. His men endured. The government that functioned now was his creation perhaps more than that of any other single man.

Lyndon Johnson, who had learned about power from Roosevelt, presided at the dedication of the portrait of FDR by Madame Elizabeth Shoumatoff, the artist who was painting Roosevelt when he was stricken in Warm Springs. There were three Roosevelt children present, a dozen grandchildren, three great-grandchildren and innumerable other relatives. But that was not the most impressive thing. What caught your interest was the number of Roosevelt counselors and staff members who still dwelt at the center of power. Besides the President there was Supreme Court Justice Abe Fortas, once an aide to Roosevelt and now one of Johnson's most trusted advisers. Thomas Corcoran, another of FDR's bright young men, was there, and he too was an occasional adviser to Johnson. James Rowe, who had been

Roosevelt's Administrative Assistant, sat in the audience. He still was a Johnson political authority. You could see Averell Harriman and Thurman Arnold in the group. It was like a great, grand reunion. They all seemed to belong there, as if the thing had been going on forever and might never stop. There was Grace Tully, who had followed Missy Lehand as Roosevelt's personal secretary. She knew everybody and they all knew her. Francis Biddle, who had been Attorney General in those good old days, looked positively patrician. Johnson had Florida's Congressman Claude Pepper stand up and he told how Pepper, when a Senator, had defended Roosevelt's foreign policy up on the Hill—a lone voice in a time of peril.

When Madame Shoumatoff pulled the gold cloth off the portrait, Johnson looked at it and said, "For me and for millions of others any likeness of this man is an inspiration. I was a new Congressional Secretary in March 1933 when Roosevelt mounted the platform and that day quoted from proverbs, 'Where there is no vision, the people perish.' This painting will, as long as I am President, hang in my office where I can see it and where I need it."

When Charlton Heston, Anne Seymour, Mary Fickett and Dore Schary read from *Sunrise at Campobello*, there were great lumps in many throats and tears collected with the memories. You watched all of them at coffee and felt the warmth in this old camaraderie and you heard the wistful laughter—almost a yearning for those days, simpler days. Then you looked out down the

242

Mall and saw the gray Federal buildings that stood there and they were monuments to that amazing man. Roosevelt had built them. It was long ago and so much had happened and yet so much was the same. There was something terribly unreal about it all, as if fate had plucked a scene from the past and dropped it into the present.

OFFICE

THE PRESIDENT'S OFFICE reflects the man. It is a functional Oval now for a functional man— Lyndon B. Johnson. The faint essence of romance that was there under John Kennedy has been swept aside and there is the smell of hard work and raw powder.

In Kennedy's time, under the expert hand of Jacqueline, the office acquired a deep historical aura flavored with New England. There were scrimshawed whales' teeth festooning the elaborate oak desk which had been carved from the beams of H.M.S. *Resolute,* a British ship abandoned in the Arctic in 1852 and later found and refitted and returned to Great Britain by the United States. In some ancient naval paintings the *Constitution* and the *Bonhomme Richard* fought their fierce encounters around the graceful walls. The visages of the founding fathers hung there too, as did such artifacts as the encrusted sword and a tattered flag once belonging to Commodore John Barry, the father of the American Navy.

Johnson is more at home among the things of his

time. His massive mahogany desk with the green leather inlay, brought from the Senate, is dominated by two telephones. The gently curving walls have been disrupted by huge white cabinets containing two news-tickers and a three-screen color television console. Above the fireplace is Franklin D. Roosevelt, the portrait by Madame Shoumatoff. Johnson can look up from his desk any time and see his friend and continuing hero. The office is a place to work, a chamber to serve the restless personality that resides there. The memorabilia are not from Commodore Barry's day but from Johnson's.

Lyndon Johnson's Presidency is a very personal Presidency. There is no manual of the Presidency, no compilation of procedures and customs which can help a novice. There is only a certain bureaucratic momentum that carries the housekeeping and protocol chores through from Administration to Administration. Each President must fashion the office to best serve his objectives. For Johnson it is singularly a one-man affair.

Of course, all the big decisions fall on the President's desk and that is what the job is all about. War and peace. Taxes and Social Security. Transportation and space. But as much minutiae will accumulate at the President's door as the man will allow. Johnson, with an incurable appetite for the minor doings of his government, for the gossipy facts about Senator and sage, busied himself at one time or another with just about everything that happened in the capital. "Not a sparrow falls in this place," said one of his White House aides, "that Johnson does not know about." He was utterly fascinated by a huge volume sent over from the Justice Department telling about the biggest tax investigations going on, and he related to friends how astounded he was at some of the names of top corporate executives and attorneys who had not paid any income tax for years. One Kennedy holdover hurried his White House departure at least in part because of Johnson's insatiable appetite for FBI dossiers on just about everybody and anybody. Johnson had the Secret Service investigate new leaks within the government, such as the one to Robert Pierpoint of CBS concerning the President's sanguine thoughts about the outcome of the 1966 primary voting. And he himself conducted unmerciful campaigns in the back corridors of the White House to squelch leaks. He knew almost instantaneously when his men were hobnobbing with the enemy. "How was dinner at Bobby's last night?" he asked one astonished Cabinet officer who had dined at Kennedy's Hickory Hill. "You think the CIA has good sources of information?" said one aide. "Johnson has better." The President got a complete rundown on which Congressmen and Senators had contact with the Soviet Embassy. He sometimes had reports on the conversations. He knew when Russian diplomats were at the swimming pool of columnist Drew Pearson or Roving Ambassador Averell Harriman. He was convinced that every flurry of sociability by the Soviets was followed by an outbreak of anti-Vietnam speeches in Congress. He got detailed FBI rundowns on pickets who

met him out around the country and, like FBI Director
J. Edgar Hoover, he felt that there was more of communist conspiracy in the United States than most people
realized. While he was flying around the world in his
great peace extravaganza in the days before Christmas
of 1967, his staff compiled a report on the complaints of
the reporters aboard the Pan American press plane.
Beside the names were listed the objections that the trip
was too fast, too secret and too tiring.

Johnson was actually quite proud of his splendid
grasp of trivia, and he firmly believed it was not irrele-
vant. It was part of the technique of governing, at least
as he knew it. To know more about the other man than
he knew about you was to be superior in any fight. Once
when he denied knowledge of the political activities of
Senator Eugene McCarthy, who became the peace candidate in December of 1967, Johnson got appreciative
chuckles from his audience. One listener ventured
good-naturedly that he couldn't take Johnson at his
word since he knew the President's ability to keep
abreast of all inside doings. LBJ was flattered. "I try to
keep informed," he said, letting a smile spread across
his face.

He held all the leads to power and he guarded all the
levers. He and he alone consigned the use. He was press
agent and bookkeeper as well as Commander-in-Chief
and campaigner. He called the Department of Health,
Education and Welfare one day to raise a little hell
because he had seen a press release issued from there
which he felt should have been put out under his name

247

at the White House. In the very early weeks of his stewardship he assembled the public-relations officers from all the departments and complained, "Well, I got a few headlines lighting the National Christmas Tree. But that's about all. What have you guys been doing?"

He went around turning off lights in the White House, showing everybody how to be frugal, until the public got weary of it. Finally, more mail arrived complaining than complimenting, so he stopped that. When at a press conference a reporter let his cigarette ashes fall on a new carpet, Johnson rushed over and scooped them up and deposited them in an ashtray. He invited newsmen into a Cabinet meeting and then held forth about the virtues of answering mail promptly and returning telephone calls in a hurry. Once down at the ranch, as he was going through the Air Force budget concerned with atomic weapons and aircraft, he spotted an item about uniforms and stopped the proceedings to command, "When you buy britches for the boys, make sure they have plenty of ball room."

The casual observer at the White House would think that all the President's time was absorbed in minor matters and ceremony. But that was not so. He immersed himself in the larger things, but he worked in these matters behind a great veil of secrecy. The gaps in his day's announced schedule were filled with the meat and potatoes of being President—long, enervating discussions of departmental budgets; the formulation of a new year's program which began almost as soon as the last message for the current year had been sent to the

Congress; detailed strategy sessions for winning the necessary support for bills in progress. To meet the demands of the Presidential office as molded by himself, Johnson worked out a two-shift day. He generally began the morning proceedings in his bedroom, sometimes as early as six or seven ("McNamara's the only Cabinet officer I can find at his desk by 7:30"), with the phone cradled on a shoulder, the TV console on for the morning news, breakfast in front of him and an aide receiving and passing memorandums. By ten or eleven he was in his office for appointments and meetings. Often he did not lunch until two or three, and then he took a nap of two or three hours. ("I sleep just as long as I want to. I wash my teeth, take a hot shower, then an ice shower.") He was back in the office or pursuing business from the family quarters until around ten or eleven, when he ate dinner, had a rubdown as he watched more news, often falling asleep three or four times during the broadcast. Frequently he would then work until one or two the next morning. The President prided himself on his ability to fall asleep instantly whenever he wanted to. "They used to kid," he said, "that Lyndon Johnson would never commit suicide. He'd fall asleep thinking about it."

He talked sparingly about the Presidency. But once he said, "You want to be very careful, apply yourself, conserve your strength, be alert and try to envision various situations here and there. . . . No man ever became President who didn't want to be the best President the country ever had. . . . I've tried hard to do right. The big problem is knowing what's right. One says, 'Full steam ahead,' and another says, 'Let's take a siesta and talk about it tomorrow.' . . . When you duck, dodge, hesitate and shimmy, every man and his dog gives you a kick. I expect to get kicked, but I don't expect to duck."

All the information flowed to him. He insisted that it be boiled down. A paragraph, a page—he saw little need for routine reports to run longer. The CIA, which had not curtailed its verbiage much, found it needed to recast its operation and put several men full-time to prepare the nightly summary for Johnson. "Look at that," said the President one night about a memorandum he had received. "I told them to put it on one page, so they have to show me who is boss." He displayed a report which had one line on a second page. From all that came his way Johnson kept what he wanted, either in his head or on his person or at his elbow. (His hot-line exchanges with Soviet boss Alexei Kosygin were elaborately bound in a green leather note book, the Russian and English versions neatly placed opposite each other within clear plastic pages.) There was no other person, really, who shared all of this with Johnson. There was something withheld from every man. Much from most. Not even Dean Rusk or Robert McNamara or Bill Moyers, when he occupied his special post of trust, had the full picture. It was another leadership tool. There was always an unknown quantity about Lyndon Johnson which kept each man from ever being totally certain what was going through the

President's mind or just how much he knew or how recent his information might be. "General Westmoreland gets a lot of information," the President once mused about his field commander's rather optimistic assessments of the fighting. "But he doesn't get the same information as Johnson, and his view is a little different."

The President saw no reason for internal conflict within a government. Instead of matching one man against another, he got rid of troublemakers. Staff rivalries were never open affairs. Grumblings about others were kept almost totally private. It was Johnson alone who was privileged to deliver the denunciations of those who worked for him. And this he did, just to keep everyone a little off balance. "That dumb bastard," he said one day about a press aide. "When you want information, come to me," he cautioned a group of reporters one night in front of his staff. "Don't go to them. They don't know what is going on." He dispensed praise with equal ease, in fact more so. "Jack Valenti knows everything I know," he once said, and another time he called him one of the finest humans in existence. No man, he said, was closer to him than Bill Moyers. Johnson, in fact, tended to overflatter his favorites. Thus, when they fell from grace or decided they had to leave government, their departure was doubly hard for Johnson to take. Bill Moyers resigned to become publisher of *Newsday* on Long Island at a reported salary of $100,000. The move hit Johnson hard. And after Moyers left, the bitterness sometimes escaped. "When Moyers became my Press Secretary, my popularity was at an all-time high and nobody ever heard of Bill Moyers. When he left, I was at an all-time low and Bill Moyers was a world hero." No civil servant received higher praise for his ability and his service than Secretary of Defense Robert McNamara. Twice Johnson asked him about becoming his Vice Presidential candidate in 1964 (both times McNamara turned him down). LBJ announced to anyone who would listen that McNamara had the best mind that he had ever encountered in government. When McNamara after six and a half years of the most grueling service decided he needed to move to another position, the realization that McNamara wanted out was a heavy blow to Johnson. "I'm not going to beg any Cabinet member to stay," he had often said. He didn't beg McNamara, and for a few confused hours in Washington it appeared that McNamara had been squeezed out. Indeed, McNamara himself may have wondered. But it was simply an old Johnson phenomenon manifesting itself once again. No man could leave Johnson gracefully, because Johnson found in every departure a bit of disloyalty.

The President could not stand it when his aides received too much publicity. He frequently was the cause, yet he did not see it that way. When a series of stories appeared about Jack Valenti as the closest aide to Johnson (mostly on Johnson's guidance) Valenti suddenly found himself physically moved a notch away from the Oval Office. The man in the office next to the President's door became Marvin Watson, a former State

Democratic Chairman of Texas and a right-leaning executive of the Lone Star Steel Company. McGeorge
Bundy's mental capacity never dimmed in the transi-
tion between Kennedy and Johnson, and LBJ was always suspicious of Bundy and never quite comfortable
with him. When the Viet Cong struck at our barracks at
Pleiku and Johnson ordered the retaliatory air raids
against North Vietnam, Bundy was in Vietnam on a
fact-finding mission, and in considerable detail the narrative told how he got on the embassy circuit and recommended a strike. Johnson was careful to note later
that "the decision for that raid was made right here in
the White House and not over there. Bundy may have
recommended the same thing, I don't know."

Little by little Johnson erased friction from his staff.
But he also lost ability. The Kennedy men all fled. And
then his own crew turned over—George Reedy, Jack
Valenti, Horace Busby, Bill Moyers, Jake Jacobson. Of
his ten top aides, six were Texans by 1968. They were
not necessarily men of lesser ability, but they were pro-
jections of Johnson. They were cautious bureaucrats,
adept at shuffling memos and doing the mechanical
things which are demanded around the White House,
but they were not given charters for original thinking.
In fact, the highly talented quartet remaining—Walt
Rostow, Joe Califano, Harry McPherson and George
Christian—were shoved into grooves that very frequently resembled ruts. The President bragged about a
youthful cadre of highly trained men, and, indeed,
there was an impressive roster. But their contribution

253

was often obscured. There was the story of the meeting of Rostow's foreign-policy group being monitored by one of Johnson's bright young men. He suddenly asked, "What's this NATO you keep talking about?"

It was virtually impossible in the Johnson Administration to trace the impact of an outside idea on the President's mind. Its origin was fogged by Johnson's own clandestine system of evaluation and his insistence on being credited with having spawned every idea which came out of his White House.

It became quite clear that there really were no nay-sayers after the departure of Moyers, who was known on a few occasions actually to have argued, "No, Mr. President, you can't do that." The Johnson partisans insisted that nay-sayers as such were not a part of the system. The President, it was said, listened eagerly to any alternatives that anyone could think up. However, after a decision was made, loyalty was demanded.

The argument made some sense. But not quite enough. George Ball became identified in the Vietnam war as the man who offered the opposition to more bombing and more escalation. However, his view rarely prevailed in his three years under Johnson. Beyond that, once a course had been set, the evidence which drifted out from these meetings indicated that nobody could have second thoughts, nor could anybody change his mind in mid-operation. At least, that was the effect of Johnson's system of government by 1968. The programs and plans laid down got almost monolithic support within the Administration. When apparent inconsistencies were spotted, as in McNamara's testimony on the Hill about the doubtful effects of the air war in North Vietnam, there were vast internal efforts by the White House to reconcile all views.

Johnson's bureaucracy worked splendidly. Papers arrived on time and reports were made. Presumably, as he had insisted, telephone calls were hurried up and mail was answered with increased efficiency. He was much pleased. "So many people want to help you, want to make your job a little easier. They're all hopeful and optimistic. They want to do something for the country they love. Very rarely do you hear a discouraging word—as the song goes." And later he would add, "I can't imagine a government in my wildest dreams functioning as efficiently as this one."

Certainly such efficiency was noteworthy. But under Johnson's rather restrictive hand, creativity diminished. Innovation was reduced. Original thought was put down in silence on paper that never floated to the surface. New ideas and new concepts cannot flourish amid total harmony. There must be a "web of tension," claimed former Ambassador Harlan Cleveland, who had watched the State Department bureaucracy for years. There has to be a grinding action. Some tempers must rise and some people must lose their battles if all points are to be considered and the necessary debate is to run its course.

Johnson never ordered that internal debate be halted. Probably he was truly irritated at the suggestion that creativity had diminished. But because the Presi-

255

dency is a very personal thing, LBJ's strong will permeated the government. The message which came through to all departments was that one man—the President, Lyndon Johnson—was to stand above all others on the landscape. His was to be the voice. Original thought—that which survived—was not to be aired until the President chose. Lassitude was inevitable under such a system.

The White House staff annually made pilgrimages to the top university campuses. Joe Califano, who had charge of assembling the domestic programs, ticked off more than a hundred top minds tapped for the 1967 planning. Yet, curiously, the thoughts of these men, truly leading authorities in their fields, were never released for public appraisal. They were assembled in a huge black notebook which was secret night reading for the President. What he took from that book eventually wound up in his programs, but very few people knew from whom the thoughts came or how much of the original concept was retained. Califano and others within the White House were quite honestly convinced that if this creative process were conducted more openly, the men who were called upon for help would not be as free and responsive with their thoughts.

He may have been correct in some instances. But I always felt that just the opposite was true. A closed and restrictive atmosphere never encouraged creativeness. No ranking academician or even industrial leader with whom I had ever been acquainted wanted his best ideas hidden under a bushel. Secrecy is not an ingredient of a

viable campus or a democracy. It defeats the prolifera-
tion of thought which is the essence of progress. Having
prepared the way for a domestic social revolution in the
early days of his Presidency, Johnson's oppressive administrative manner unfortunately helped inhibit its
fulfillment.

The arguments about the power dimensions of the
Presidency went on throughout Johnson's first four
years with, predictably, no sound conclusion. There
never has been. Each President must cast his own
shadow. The strong men have seized all the power they
could get and have used it as they saw fit. Sometimes
they were challenged and defeated, as Harry Truman
was in his seizure of the railroads and the steel mills.
Lincoln assumed more power than the Constitution
granted him, but a nation craving national leadership
in its darkest hour did not question him until he had
restored the Union. Johnson has never transgressed in
such obvious fashion. Indeed, he has been particularly
careful of Congress' rights and customs in all areas but
that of foreign policy, which is considered in these times
to be almost the exclusive preserve of the President.
The parameters of power in foreign affairs have always
been ill defined, and the amount of power which a
President can exercise directly has depended on the
man and his era. In the nuclear age a Chief Executive
must have the power for instantaneous and shattering
response.

The growing dissent about the Vietnam war triggered controversy over the powers of the Presidency.

257

Chief among the questioners was the Senate's J. William Fulbright, embittered by the rejection of his advice at the White House ("The stud duck of the opposition," Johnson said). In some inconclusive hearings by the Foreign Relations Committee he questioned "the overextension of executive powers." A particular thorn to Fulbright was the Gulf of Tonkin Resolution which Johnson won from Congress in the summer of 1964. Designed to back the President's aerial retaliation against North Vietnam after torpedo boats had attacked our destroyers, the resolution was unwisely trotted out by Johnson at every opportunity from then on and waved as a full Congressional endorsement of the war. There was ill-temper on both sides. The Administration made it quite clear when it sought the resolution that it was for more than just the response to the torpedo-boat attacks. Any responsible legislator knew by that time that the Vietnam situation was increasingly tense and complex and that American involvement would grow before it would diminish. That very point was debated on the floor. Johnson, on the other hand, went through the subsequent 1964 campaign declaring that he did not want American boys fighting that war for the Asians. When American boys were sent to fight, Johnson produced the Gulf of Tonkin Resolution as his authority. It rang hollowly. He carried that, too, in his inside coat pocket for months. He would take it out and read it to his audiences. The vote of 485 to 2 was his charter to wage the largest conflict in United States history without a declaration of war from Congress. This was at the core of the problem.

On at least 125 occasions in United States history Presidents have intervened abroad without Congressional approval. Jefferson dispatched a naval force to war against the Barbary pirates in 1801. He did not seek Congressional approval. Polk sent forces to skirmish with the Mexicans in Texas, Franklin Roosevelt ordered troops to Iceland and, of course, Truman responded to Korean aggression. Ike intervened in Lebanon, and Kennedy in the Cuban missile crisis. Johnson was doing something similar.

Yet there was justification for wondering about the legal grounds for a war that in terms of manpower had topped the Korean engagement (472,800 vs. 525,000) and was costing some $30 billion a year and was threatening to become, by about any measurement, the longest war in our history. The questioning, however, was prompted more by sheer frustration about the war than by any real desire to have the nation plunged into a state of national emergency, as the Republican hopeful Ronald Reagan suggested, or to limit the power of the President. Most thoughtful students of the Presidency, while not necessarily endorsing Johnson's Vietnam decisions, recognized the necessity of the President having and exercising the power to do what he had done.

In fact, Johnson was much concerned about violating Constitutional rights. In the Detroit riots in the summer of 1967 he waited so long to establish a legal base before sending troops to help out Governor George Romney that he could be justly criticized for being too concerned. Most of the practicing politicians agreed in the end with Harry Truman's old assessment: "The Presidency is exactly as powerful as it was under George Washington." Neither Nelson Rockefeller nor Richard Nixon nor even Ronald Reagan worried much about the arguments of the academicians over the concentration of power and its use by the President. The system had not been impaired. In the end, it was the man and how he chose to use that power.

Johnson talked remarkably little about the powers of the office. He once said that he did not intend to "preside over its erosion. I intend to turn over the office with all of its powers intact to the next man who sits in this chair." In his days of adversity he was sometimes convinced that those powers did not amount to much. "Power?" he said. "The only power I've got is nuclear—and I can't use that." Harry Truman had the same misgivings, noting at the end of a trying day that all he seemed to do was "spend most of my time kissing somebody's ass."

In the final analysis, the suggestions that Johnson had abused his Constitutional authority just did not hold up. Instead, Johnson's problem seemed to be, as noted before, that he had not used skillfully those intangible powers which accompany the Presidency—education and inspiration. He failed in critical moments to carry the country along with him, to establish the broad base of support which was necessary for achievement. He did not enlighten; he promised. He did not inspire; he threatened.

The Presidency continued to grow. Its most important expansion was in foreign affairs, where the Commander-in-Chief of the United States armed forces became the single most important figure in the stability of the world. Stanford's Historian Emeritus Edgar E. Robinson suggested that "the growth of the powers of the President in foreign relations appears to be the most important phenomenon in modern history."

In domestic matters there was built-in expansion directly relating to the size of the American population. Beyond that, the most important enlargement of the Presidency in the Johnson years was in the economy. Indisputably, the President became the nation's chief economist. The tax cut of 1964 spurred the economy to an all-time expansion record. His hesitation in seeking a tax increase to damp the economy in 1966 caused some serious doubts that brought economic tremors later. Government purchasing could bring prosperity or depression to certain cities and regions. Whole industries, such as the aircraft industry, were dependent on defense orders. Johnson stood firmly behind the new trade agreements hammered out in 1967, and he issued a strong warning against the protectionist sentiment that began to build in the Congress toward the end of the year. To quell the gold drain and the continuing deficit in our balance of payments, he proposed restrictions on foreign travel and overseas business investment.

Each year the budget became a national economic road map. The Federal government at the close of 1967 was taking $130 billion in taxes out of a gross national product of $800 billion. Almost every word the President spoke and most of his actions in some way bore on the economy. A few years ago there were still industrialists who could ignore the White House. There are few, if any, left. One financial writer received calls from five industrial economists seeking advance information about Johnson's budget one year, an astounding reversal of the old custom where government went on its knees to industry.

The majesty of the Presidency matched the power. There was no office in the world to rival its grandeur in the twentieth-century sense. "Don't feel sorry for me," said the President after he had held office for a few months. "I'm treated better than any of you. I'm the only guy here who didn't have to work today. I worked because I wanted to. I'm thinking about the guy who's not working this week for General Motors [a strike was in progress]. He doesn't have pretty secretaries and Cadillacs and everything done for him." Most of the personal wants of the President were tended to by a butler, seventeen house servants (and others when needed), a limitless fleet of chauffeured limousines, a masseur, a resident physician and all the secretaries needed. Anybody else who was required rushed to the White House on signal.

Johnson loved it all, although sometimes he feebly protested. "We're not royal highnesses. I don't want to be king. I just want to see people. . . . All day long they call me Mr. President. I wish they'd just call me Lyndon sometimes. . . . When I was Senate leader I used to work twenty-four hours a day and I had visions of dying on the Senate floor. As Vice President, I worked even harder. But as President, I can devote my full energy to problems of guys like 'old Joe' who come down to Washington with three days off and want to see the President. I just try to be accommodating."

The jet airplane became an extension of the Oval Office, allowing the President to see any of his constituents in forty-eight of the fifty states within one day's time and get back to the White House by night. Johnson used it to the limit. He spent 58 hours in the air during his trip around the world at Christmastime in 1967. The trip totaled 116 hours. The average speed for every hour of that journey was 225 miles. A Johnson jet trip was a ballet of power and motion. No other head of government could command such service. From his office Johnson could simply walk through the Rose Garden to a waiting helicopter. When the President was twenty-five yards from the chopper, the pilot started the jet engine. As Johnson buckled his seat belt, the craft lifted off. Below, the cars on the streets behind the White House were halted as Johnson passed overhead on his way to Andrews Air Force Base and the big jet that waited for him. As the chopper landed, Colonel James Cross, the President's military aide and pilot, started the starboard wing engines. As LBJ entered the fuselage, the two engines on the port side came to life. It was calculated that the taxi to the head of the runway took approximately three and a half minutes. The big ship lifted off the ground just twenty-two seconds after it began its takeoff run. There was no guesswork. Colonel Cross carried no rabbit's foot or good-luck medal. Runways were blocked off for five minutes for takeoffs and landings. Aloft, the skyways were swept clean of other planes as Air Force One sped to its destination. The ship was in constant radio and radar contact. When it was over water, there were picket ships or planes every hundred miles in case of emergency. On the ground the President only had to walk down the ramp and get into a waiting limousine (generally his own special car, which had been ferried ahead in another jet) and drive to his destination over streets that had been cleared for him.

The city that Johnson occupied was far different from the place he had come to as a Congressman. Long ago it gave up its claim of being a rather sleepy Southern bastion in which the Congress merely encamped for a few weeks and which was run by the encrusted commercial families. It was in postwar years governmental, a company town. Kennedy made it a Presidential town. And it was kept that way by the sheer force of events in Johnson's Presidency. He could hardly have cared less. He was in some ways a stranger in its streets. It is doubtful that he could have found his way through Georgetown or that he knew a half-dozen good restaurants. He stayed where the power was. Yet the mood of Washington was set by Johnson. And it was not always a happy place. The artistry of living at once meaningfully and pleasurably was not a Johnson talent. Elegance fled. The sounds of after-hours gaiety faded. Johnson's capital was one of working men and women. Johnson decreed that his men were not to waste their time at cocktail parties and that accomplishment was to be the only order of life. Cowboys and evangelists, Rotarians and industrialists set the beat of the Great Society, which in quantity proved itself but never could achieve the quality that Johnson wanted.

There was too little enjoyment in Washington. The youthful society over which Jackie Kennedy had presided broke up, and there was nothing at the White House to replace it. Johnson simply did not care. His entertaining was business—visiting kings, queens, presidents and prime ministers. It was out of necessity, not out of desire. Legislator was preferred over artist, teacher over philosopher, draftsman over dreamer and, really, dinner at the desk over crêpes at the French embassy.

Now and then Johnson could shed his dour mantle. At a State Dinner for Denmark's Prime Minister Jens Otto Krag he was swept up in the pleasantry and danced to the music of Lee Evans until three a.m., his own enthusiasm infecting the White House and bringing the ultimate compliment from the beauteous Mrs. Krag: "It's the best party of my life. And I'm going to tell King Frederick." But always something down inside Johnson would reach up and reclaim him and the glow would fade in a few hours.

The French chef whom Jackie had installed in the kitchen found that he could not live under the stern handling of the housekeeper whom Johnson had brought up from Austin's Driskill Hotel. "These things you just don't do to a respectable chef," sputtered René Verdon when he resigned. "You don't ask a chef to serve red snapper with the skin still on it, beets with cream all over them. Look, I have a master pastry chef who has been doing yule logs for forty years. You just don't open the *Gourmet Cookbook* to page forty and stick it under his eyes. I've tried to cooperate. I've tried to get along. But I've reached the end of the line."

Johnson could not easily laugh at himself. And so there was little humor in Washington. It comes much harder to men like Johnson who have seen deprivation and fought for everything they possess than it does to others like Kennedy. There was rarely time in Johnson's life, which centered on the Great Depression, for him to discover and learn to appreciate the subtle pleasures of sight and sound and taste. There is one place such men feel at home—in the workrooms.

The war inevitably dampened the spirit of the city. On those few nights when good times prevailed either at the White House or beyond, there was almost always a guilty conscience the next day. At the opera ball in the Smithsonian Institution Bill Moyers took a rare night off and did something resembling a frug on the dance floor. His mistake was to allow a photograph, which appeared the next day on front pages across the country. Outraged mail rolled in to the Congress, and such guardians of the public morals as Iowa's sixty-six-year-old bluenose, H. R. Gross, took to their feet in indignation. "I am old-fashioned enough to be shocked, too, at these orgies," a New Yorker wrote Gross, who promptly inserted the letter in the *Congressional Record*. "They remind me of what I've read of the Roman Empire." This was a warning to Johnson. He restricted even his White House dancing, which was a discreet fox trot. While men died in Vietnam there could not be obvious revelry along the Potomac. The tragedy was that a good deal of the spirit of this youthful nation was curtailed. And that spirit was desperately needed in the capital.

Some of Johnson's suspicions of Washington were justified. The city acquired a Byzantine flavor in the 1960's. It was almost like the Vatican, a state within a state. No longer did it draw its flavor from the rest of the country. Congressmen became year-round residents. Their families settled in Chevy Chase or Arlington, and they lived out their lives in these comfortable suburbs. The vast hordes of the bureaucracy whom Franklin Roosevelt had brought to town thirty years before peopled the metropolitan area. Washington was an end in itself. Congressmen and Senators soon forgot their regional loyalties. Their object was to dwell in the society of official Washington, to rise in the power structure that dictated status and education and income. One of the first things the wife of the newly elected Indiana Senator Birch Bayh said was, "I've always wanted to live in Washington." Anticipation of arriving overwhelmed regret at leaving. Pierre Salinger, Kennedy's Press Secretary, went to California to run for the Senate so he could come back to Washington. He did not succeed. But Bobby Kennedy did in New York. Kennedy performed well for his state. But his eye was on the Presidency, and Washington was the place for a man with such grand ambitions to be.

The city became possessed with itself. And in that way it became provincial. The correspondents were incestuous, feeding on each other. The feel of the nation was left to pollsters. The resident pundits raised themselves to kingly status. Too often what they said was without basis in fact, but because they were big names in a news-conscious town they were lionized by a collection of tinsel intellectuals and society matrons on the make. ("There are a lot of these Washington hostesses that want to be invited to social events and they are sore that the White House is no longer a place for parties," Johnson once accurately observed.)

The city developed its sacred rites—the Gridiron spoofs, the Georgetown candlelight dinners, the early-morning tennis games. Its high priests were Walter Lippmann and Dean Acheson. In the atmosphere of paper and talk, a lot of its masculinity washed away. Few of the people, once they got to Washington, ever again smelled a stockyard or saw a blast furnace or watched a farmer break earth in a lonely field. Before the old bomber pilot Curt LeMay fled the place, he took out his cigar, stared across the beautiful valley cradling the capital and snorted, "I hate it. It's run by women." Lyndon Johnson's thoughts were not far from that.

Whatever the cause, after four Johnson years the city

did not give its number-one resident much of itself. Johnson's isolation was greater than ever. The eighteen acres of the White House drifted like an island in hostile water. Suspicion surrounded the place, and Johnson in turn was deeply mistrustful of most of the people beyond the high iron fences. He blurted one night to an aide who had erred, "I can't trust anybody. What are you trying to do to me? Everybody is trying to cut me down, destroy me."

His withdrawal was a natural phenomenon of the Presidency. It happened to Roosevelt, Truman and Kennedy. The battering from outside gets so intense that the man in the Oval Office surrounds himself with those who approve of what he is doing and reassure him that he is right. Johnson's circle of top-level advisers first shrank to five. They were Rusk and McNamara, Washington Attorney Clark Clifford and Supreme Court Justice Abe Fortas, HEW Secretary John Gardner. And then, with the departure of McNamara and Gardner, there were only three men who had that vital intimacy with the President which can influence policy. Sometimes it seemed that Johnson really was unaffected by any outside counsel. It was as if he had established the blueprint of his Administration, in both domestic and international affairs; that he had proved to himself the correctness of the design and would devote all his energy, whether for one or five years, to making his plan work.

IMPRESSION

IT WAS THE big Hereford sale down at Blanco County Fair Grounds just outside of Johnson City in December of 1966. And the Old Boys, as San Antonio *Express* Farm and Ranch Editor Arthur Moczygemba calls them, were all bringing in their bulls in the morning for judging for the sale that afternoon. The sale is an annual event sponsored by the Blanco County Hereford Association, of which Dale Malechek, the foreman of the LBJ Ranch, was president that year. There is no more enthusiastic Hereford man around, of course, than Lyndon Johnson, and he's missed only one of the sales in recent years. Because if there is anything in this world which provides him with more pleasure than passing bills, it is going to a Hereford sale with the sounds and the sights and smells of good cattle and the camaraderie of ranchers.

Johnson wasn't about to tell anybody that he was going to the sale. "He just figured," said one of his men who knew the secret plans, "that he wasn't going to go down there with his press following along and disrupt the sale. Those ranchers wouldn't like that."

The morning judging was done splendidly by C. R.

Landon, Jr., of Houston. And you might have known that the President's two-year-old bull LBJ Husker Design 26, which weighed in at a solid 1,770 pounds, would be judged the best in the singles. Some of the skeptical might say that it was because of the prominence of the owner. But that wasn't it, the old boys insist. "They just couldn't care less if he was President or not," said one of them. "Ole Linton [it comes out that way at a Hereford sale] has some pretty good cattle now. He didn't use to. But he's got some pretty good blood there now like Mill Iron 13 and Silver Mischief 48. These old boys were buying for stock, not for the President."

They finished the judging down at the pens behind the show ring in the morning and then everybody had a lunch and plenty of hot coffee because it was a little chilly and then they waited for the big sale in the white auction barn at one p.m. There was something a little strange about it because the sale didn't get started right at one. Hereford sales as a rule are prompt. The old boys know that. About four hundred of them were sitting there on the raw lumber bleachers that rise in a semicircle around the sawdust show pit. "Let's go!" they started yelling, putting their boots up on the railing, tipping back their Texas hats. They had money, and cattle were up, so they wanted action.

Colonel Walter Britten, the raw-lunged auctioneer, had been tipped off that Johnson was coming to the sale, and he was not saying a word, just holding back a bit, fiddling around like he had something to do that was delaying the chant. The Colonel is a mountain of a man—six feet two inches tall, 220 pounds, every bit as massive as Lyndon. He's known all over the Southwest as a cattle auctioneer. He sells Winthrop Rockefeller's Herefords over in Arkansas. The Colonel was standing on his raised platform that looked like a pulpit down on the sawdust, and he was waiting. And then all of a sudden he got the signal and he lit into it, as he remembered it later. "Here comes the champion animal of the offering consigned by the LBJ Ranch . . . now, what am I bid?"

LBJ Husker Design 26 came lumbering into the pit with Dale Malechek leading him on a halter. Husker was a handsome animal, indeed—big, blocky and virile. The old boys fixed their eyes on him because this was their business, and only a few of them noticed a small party of men who came in at the top of the auction stands and turned and sat down on the last seat. There was the number-one old boy of Blanco County himself, Lyndon B. Johnson. He had on his cowboy boots and his rancher's twill, but he didn't have a Texas hat. Judge A. W. Moursund, looking just as solid as the bull, was along, and some other friends. So was Lady Bird, sort of feminine and colorful in a fall suit. The only men in the party who looked a little conspicuous were the Secret Service agents in their Eastern-cut suits, their hip guns bulging underneath their Italian vents.

The Colonel sometimes gets a bid right off and then things move smoothly. He kind of expected to get $1,000, but maybe because of the name LBJ the ranch-

ers were a little hesitant on this one, so he had no takers
at first. The bull was a good one and $1,000 would have
been normal and right, but the men waited. So the
Colonel knew what to do and he "real hurriedly," as he
reconstructed it, started in at $500. That was low
enough to get some interest. It went to $600, then $700
and $850 and by then the heat was beginning to build.
The Colonel had slipped into high gear and nobody but
the serious ranchers knew what he was saying. He was
rattling along and he looked up and he noticed for one
split second that Lady Bird was having the time of her
life, far away from the White House and society obliga-
tions and beauty parlors and dressmakers. She was
caught up in that chant and she was smiling and laughing and having a time of it, leaning over and talking
excitedly to her friends. The Colonel worked Husker
right on up once he had thawed the old boys out. He
got the price to $1,700 and he began working mightily
to hit $2,000. He had figured that if he got the animal
to $1,500 he was in clover from there on out and he
probably could run on up a few more hundred. "Now
you're looking at an excellent animal," he cried, slow-
ing that machine-gun verbiage down just a bit. "Com-
parable animals have brought $2,000 around here in
recent sales." He talked it up that way for two or three
minutes, then he got the feel of things and he quick
calculated that he had taken Husker just as far as he
would go, so he whacked the gavel down hard and
roared, with just a little extra basso, "Sold!" Ole Lyndon grinned a mile, as the Colonel noted, because it was

273

a pretty good price. The McBride Hereford Ranch of
Llano bought the bull. And no sooner had Husker
waddled out of the show ring than the Colonel was
swinging into the next sale. There was still more Johnson action to come. He had LBJ Husker Design M12 to
sell off, a lesser bull to be sure but still good stock and,
more important, good fun. The bidding on that one
started slow and went up at $10 a crack. But it got even
hotter than the other. The old boys began to raise their
hands, signaling their bids. Arthur Moczygemba was
down there on the floor taking bids and he was watching for the flick of a wrist. Arthur is just a bit of a
showman himself, and when one of the men would give
him a bid he would turn to him and shout again,
"Yeahhhhhhhh!" The President got to enjoying it so
much that he was leaning over and slapping the old
boys on the back and talking and laughing like he'd
never heard of the White House. The bull topped out
at $650, the third-highest price of the thirty-eight-bull
sale, and he went to John Nash of Austin.

Some Future Farmers of America, downy-cheeked
boys in their blue jackets, came clattering in and took
seats across from Lyndon, but they hardly even saw that
he was a President. It was just a good country sale.
Johnson stayed on awhile after Lady Bird left. He was
in some kind of promised land without press corps and
cameras, just among friends and animals. Down in the
ring Arthur was keeping his eye on LBJ. "Funny
thing," said Arthur afterward, "he didn't do any waving
while he was in there. Brother, if he had waved, I'd

274

have taken that bid from him." Only when Johnson got up to leave did he give a little wave, sort of thanks to the old boys. He walked out happy as a rancher could be. Besides the bulls, he had sold eleven heifers, which was a pretty good score for a slow Monday down in old Johnson City, which, as Lady Bird likes to say, "is our hearts' home."

DECISION

H OW ATROPHIED LYNDON JOHNSON'S
GOVERNMENT HAD BECOME, how much
a one-man affair it was, how jealously he kept his counsel even from his most intimate advisers and friends,
was shown on March 31, 1968, when he went before a
nationwide television audience and on that Sunday
night announced a partial bombing pause over North
Vietnam, a new emphasis on South Vietnam's part in
the war and then, stunning the nation, the fact that he
would not seek or accept the Democratic nomination for
another term.

His change of war plans had, indeed, been discussed
by his inner circle. But most of the government had
been kept in the dark, and only a few days earlier responsible men were cautioning that this was not the
time to stop the bombing—not while our men were en-
dangered around the Demilitarized Zone.

Johnson's decision not to run for another term had
also been discussed with a tight little band of friends.
But it was not really believed except by a handful. And

in the final seconds as Johnson finished his prepared text, reading from the video machines in his floodlighted office, the men who had helped with the decision and his statement, Christian and Busby, were not sure that he would finally renounce the power. Even his wife was not entirely certain.

Just an hour or so before he went on the air he had told his men, "I'm not going to know, probably, until I get in there whether I'm going to use that speech." He had prepared a similar statement of retirement for use at the end of the State of the Union message in January, but he had decided against it in the final minutes. Clark Clifford, who had been named Secretary of Defense to replace McNamara, and others had listened to Johnson's musings about not running, but they simply did not believe him. Busby and Christian took him almost at his word, but they knew also his great inner relish of power and the unpredictability of the man. So did Lady Bird.

Only when Johnson paused that night, looked over at Lady Bird, raised his hand as if to brush drops of sweat from his forehead, halted the action and laid his hand down, then turned his eyes back to the cue machine and began to read were those in the Oval Office certain that the President would go through with his drastic plans.

Even in this moment of the highest political drama, disbelief in the President and what he said was so intense that a sizable segment of the people refused to believe Johnson meant to retire. His action was considered by these persons to be some super-sinister plot whose complexity was such that nobody could fathom it but whose outcome would be Johnson's nomination by popular demand. Some suspected that he had secret communications from Hanoi indicating the Viet Cong wanted peace and that, acting on this advance assurance, Johnson had staged another of his spectacles, hoping to regain popularity. Evidence that his action was so totally selfish was missing. Likewise, there were no facts to support the recurrent story that his health was failing.

It is impossible to find your way through the labyrinth of Johnson's mind. But brief hindsight suggests that Johnson, as usual, acted from a mixture of emotions and convictions. If he had not been the beleaguered leader he was at the start of 1968, he would not have announced his plans to climb down from that marvelous pedestal of power. But he was in trouble. For the good of the nation—perhaps, even for the world—and for the good of himself and his rating in history, he decided that his time was up.

In this decision, as in others, Johnson was many persons within himself. Each was carefully shielded from the rest. There was foremost the man concerned for his nation. The dimensions of the national disunity had at last dawned upon Johnson. It is doubtful that he accepted his full share of the responsibility for that. He recognized, as he told broadcasting executives in Chicago the day after his television address, that he had a communication problem. But he seemed to believe that it was wholly a mechanical thing—how he looked on TV, what words he spoke, where and when he showed up. There is no evidence that he realized that by failing to put his full faith in the people, by conducting the affairs of a democracy in his secretive fashion, he had foreclosed receiving trust from the nation. He recognized that the events of his time—the war in Vietnam, the gold crisis, race riots and crime—were gigantically erosive by themselves. But he seemed not to sense that his own lack of candor about these events amplified their evil effects on the country. Nevertheless, his realization of the divisiveness was genuine, and more than anything else it disheartened him as he approached the decisive year 1968.

Before Christmas, flying around the world on his peace mission, he summoned Busby to his cabin aboard Air Force One as that jet rushed from Pakistan into Christmas Eve in Rome, and he talked about the disunity and his desire to step out of office at the end of his term, to somehow bring the country back together again. He was the President of consensus, and proud of it. He had tried, above all else, to weld the country together, but the evidence was there for all to see that in these final months he was not succeeding. The solution, as he saw it, was to take himself out of national life. Busby agreed. Johnson reasoned that as a President unburdened by politics he would be more apt to be believed. As a non-candidate he could devote all his time to the pursuit of peace, both in the streets of the United States and in Vietnam. This was Lyndon Johnson, the President of all the people. There was a lot of that small boy from Johnson City declaiming about the flag flying simple and proud in foreign lands.

There was a person inside Johnson who was worried

about what history would say about his quitting his office after sending half a million men halfway around the world to fight and die for a cause which was cursing the country and which Johnson could not explain to the people's total satisfaction. Time was running out on that person. He had to make his decision so that he would have time left in his term to seriously seek the peace he professed to want, thus convincing the historians of his selflessness in the act. His decision not to seek another term was in its way an admission of the failure of leadership, but it was an admission he never really had to state publicly because he chose a time and circumstances that cast it in the best light. Had it come earlier, he might have been called a coward by those who wished to bomb and burn even more. Had it come later, he might have been labeled a man who did not have the strength of his convictions.

Finally, there was a very personal person inside Johnson. That was the man who told himself that he could be happy back in Texas looking at his cattle, rummaging through his papers in the new Lyndon B. Johnson Library planned at the University of Texas, maybe teaching a class or two in government ("Devising those plans that nobody can execute") and always ready to serve as a special envoy to anywhere. It was a pleasant dream. It was Lady Bird's dream, and she had worked subtly to get him back there before his life ran out on him. Johnson wanted to enjoy those millions of dollars he had accumulated, to see more of his daughters and their families, to be "like an animal in the forest, go sleep under a tree, eat when I feel like it, read a bit, and, after a while, do whatever I want to do." His new grandson, Patrick Lyn Nugent, whom he adored and proudly displayed when he could, was a stimulant for more family life.

The President had withdrawal pains. In the immediate hours after his announcement he bitterly denounced his worst critics. He flailed the press, once again heaping most of the blame for his credibility problems on reporters and broadcasters. He showed equal scorn for his Senate adversaries, such as Fulbright. Of course Bobby Kennedy was castigated; sometimes in his musings Johnson retraced the steps of his own Vice Presidency, when he had given John F. Kennedy total loyalty, and he always posed for his listeners the tacit question of why Bob Kennedy did not return the favor. "We need a Churchill in this country now," Johnson said one afternoon. He worried aloud about the pressures of the office. "The load is unbearable . . . you have to have the physical constitution of a mule and great dedication." He had been unable to unite the country, he continued, or even Congress, and the criticism had focused more and more on him. Everything he did was suspect. He couldn't put out the Lord's Prayer without criticism. He had become like barnacles on a ship. He was "the coach everyone was trying to shoot."

But just when self-pity seemed about to overwhelm him, he would veer the conversation back again to the main line. "I have to say to the Communist world that this man has nothing to gain. And when I do that, they have to say he is credible. . . . If I can't do any good this way, I just guess I can't do any good."

There was in his rumination some evidence that he still carried that Texas chip on his shoulder. It was not, perhaps, as big as it used to be, but it was still there. "For a Johnson City boy, I've gone about as far as I can go and done a pretty good job," he said. And later, when he was quiet and thoughtful for a moment, he added, "I don't need the salary and I don't need the job. . . . I don't particularly give a damn what they think about it." He was, at least for the moment, going back where he came from, and there was some of that old feeling that the world had been unjust and unappreciative and so to hell with it. Mostly Johnson was bigger than that. What had been coming—what he finally did—may have been inevitable. Perhaps he was ahead of his time in sensing it. Maybe, as he firmly believed, there was nothing else he could have done to stave off disunity except surrender his convictions.

Historians can argue in later years just how much Johnson was responsible for the tide of events that eventually engulfed him. The fact was that the battering the President received in the first months of 1968 was as severe as that suffered by any President since the Civil War. He claimed that just as soon as he was inaugurated in 1964 he had contemplated stepping out after a single term. Certainly over his years in the Presidency, and even before, there had been that constant questioning of the adequacy of his own background. I remember standing with Johnson on his ranch land in the spring of 1960, looking at the bluebonnets and other Texas wildflowers cascading down those hillsides, and being startled as he seemed almost to be talking to some invisible audience before him about himself. At that time he felt he had a chance to get the Democratic nomination and he wanted to be President. But there was a doubt, a small dark cloud on his expansive horizon. "I know I've got a heart big enough to be President," he said suddenly, looking far away. "I know I've got guts enough to be President. But I wonder whether I've got intelligence and ability enough to be President—I wonder if any man does."

Throughout his Presidency he worried privately and publicly about his Texas background. He wondered if a man so regionally identified could bring about the unity he craved. On board his 1964 campaign jet he said, "I'd probably be a lot happier if I did lose. Luci's here, Lynda's the other place and Lady Bird's off somewhere. I could go back to the ranch and live comfortably. We'd have more after taxes and I could shoot my deer without having the Humane Society after me." His doubts came out in different ways at different times—complaints sometimes about intellectuals and their intolerance, resentment of the Georgetown drawing-room set, alienation from the Harvard contingent. He brooded about the credibility problem and where it was leading him and his administration. Yet, all of this was not untypical Johnson behavior. He had always complained about the lack of appreciation which people showed for his talents. His relish of the Presidency, particularly when he was successful in getting the legislation he wanted, was plain to see. Before the fall of 1967 his peevishness and his black moments of self-doubt were put down to self-pity.

Perhaps the most profound influence in the early stages of his decision came from those closest to him—Lady Bird and his best friend, John Connally. Mrs. Johnson wanted him to have some years back at the ranch, as she wanted them for herself. She truly feared that he would not live out another term. Her approach was not frontal—she knew the man too well. Subtly she urged him to be his own judge, to make up his own mind. But she was a passionate advocate of the glories of a rancher's life, a reminder of the decades he already had given to public service, a wife who wanted to see the end of the power road and to savor her family.

In the fall of 1967 when John Connally told the President that he did not want to run for a third term as Texas Governor unless the President felt he needed him in the race, Johnson turned seriously to the consideration of his own position. One day in October, at the ranch, George Christian was summoned by the President to take down his ideas about retiring. Christian scribbled on a yellow legal tablet as Johnson thought out loud, forming the rudimentary outlines of a statement which he could include in a speech. LBJ wanted to review the course he had set in the Vietnam war, to explain again the need to stand fast and uphold the United States' word. He wanted also, in such a statement, to go over his plans for the nation and point out that, even though there were many problems, much progress had been made. He told Christian that he should say the time had come to choose priorities. He did not feel that he could indulge the time and energy for a national political campaign and still be the President he felt he should be in these tense times. For fourteen months he wanted to give his total attention to the pursuit of peace abroad and unity at home. Nobody was indispensable, he said. Christian wrote all this down and then, on the President's instructions, drove to Austin to go over the ideas with Connally. The two men walked in the garden of the Governor's house, which Nelly Connally was having renovated. Then they settled at the dining-room table and Connally did much the same as Johnson had done, while Christian wrote on small pieces of White House stationery. Momentum began building from that moment. Johnson hurried toward his decision, and yet there was always the feeling that he might be pulled back by favorable events. None developed.

The divisiveness in the country increased. That rhythmic optimism that had held the nation's interest for two years, in anticipation of peace talks or a spectacular collapse of the enemy just around the corner, began to wear thin. The talks did not develop. The victory did not come. The size of the war began to horrify many. Casualties exceeded those of the Korean conflict. Bomb tonnage surpassed that dumped on Europe in World War II. It was the third-longest war in our history, and the total cost threatened to equal that of World War II.

Minnesota's Senator Eugene McCarthy decided to become a candidate for the Democratic nomination, not

285

expecting to win the nomination but wishing to open the country for a national debate about the course Johnson was following. Johnson's hand on Washington and the government and the policy-making process by then was more oppressive than even some of Johnson's critics realized. Dissent had been totally eliminated from his staff and close advisers. Dean Rusk bluntly told visitors there were no new ideas. Johnson himself seemed mired in this bog, unable or unwilling to experiment. He kept the pressure on the enemy, gently notching it up in the pattern which he had established back in 1965. Walt Rostow's charts showed impressive kill ratios and capture of enemy weapons. To the White House, victory seemed within reach. But war is a bottomless pit. More men were needed. So was more money. Hanoi remained silent. McCarthy went ahead with his plans to enter the primaries and let some Americans cast a ballot on their feelings.

Meanwhile Johnson consulted General Westmoreland about the effect that a withdrawal by him would have on the troops. Westmoreland, back for consultation, said it would be a shock at first but that the men would get over it. Johnson grew more convinced that his time was up. He dropped those hints that nobody believed. When Ev Dirksen came around for a drink one evening and the talk got to politics, the President looked at his old friend and said, "I'm not a candidate for anything." Dirksen pondered the significance of that remark and wondered if Johnson was ready to get out of the White House. But he, like others, was not ready to take the

President at his word. Johnson in these weeks used to prod his staff about the programs on which they were at work. "We've only a few more months to get this done," he said time after time. In public he talked as though his time would be up in 1968, but everybody thought that was only shrewd politics, the humility that a proper candidate must show. In the quiet moments Lady Bird kept up her effective war, reminding the President periodically that he should allow time to let the people know if he was not going to run.

Bobby Kennedy brooded. He had declared himself out, and he began to wonder in the fall of 1967 if he had not made a mistake. When McCarthy declared, Kennedy was even more introspective. He could not calculate a way at that time by which he could take the nomination away from Johnson. Unlike McCarthy, he did not wish to run "to create a national dialogue." Kennedy still reckoned that his best time was 1972. Yet he was deeply troubled. Politics is not often a waiting game. Opportunities have to be carved out. The times and the man and the conditions rarely fit perfectly. Opportunity must be seized even if it is not ideal. To procrastinate in national politics is so often to be left behind. Beyond that was Kennedy's genuine alarm about the condition of the country and the steady escalation in the war. He was nearly convinced that four more years of Lyndon Johnson in the White House would be a national disaster. He wondered to himself and to those close around him whether he should not take the long shot. In the fall and winter of 1967, however, the political mathematics were too much against him. He continued to declare himself out.

Events—the ultimate arbiters of politics—accumulated against Johnson. As 1968 began, Congress was even more truculent than before. There was no indication that it was any more ready for the ten-percent income surtax which Johnson had requested than the year before, when no action had been taken. The pinch in funds forced Johnson to present a plan for the year devoid of any major new program. It was to be a year of austerity. The second of Johnson's two Cabinet appointees from outside the government, John Gardner, quit at least in part because he could not get the necessary funds to battle the social ills which he saw growing more menacing than ever. Great Britain devalued its pound and, in anticipation that the United States might have to do the same, a run on the London gold market began.

The Communists launched their New Year (Tet) offensive, ripping to shreds the optimistic predictions of Westmoreland and Ambassador Bunker about the year ahead. Those "secure" populated areas suddenly became battlegrounds. The American Embassy was attacked by a suicide squad, which blasted a hole in the concrete wall and penetrated into the building before being wiped out. In the major cities there were coordinated and effective attacks. The pacification program ground to a halt as troops were rushed to the cities for the bloody house-to-house fighting. Lyndon Johnson and the others within the White House were deeply shaken despite the testimony of the generals and diplomats that the offensive might be a last-gasp effort by the Viet Cong to turn the situation to its favor before negotiating.

There was no let-up in the chain of dismal events. The electronic snooping ship *Pueblo* and her crew were captured by the North Koreans and this nation was powerless to do anything except object diplomatically. The ship, clearly operating in international waters, had no protective escort either in the air or on the sea. The piracy was so unexpected and so swift that no effective rescue operation or retaliation could be ordered. Lyndon Johnson sadly followed the episode and knew that there was nothing he could do. Speaking of the dirty game of spying, he said one night in his small study, "If you are going to play in a pigpen, you are going to get dirty now and then."

Fighting continued to rage in Vietnam, and Johnson dispatched General Earle Wheeler for a new assessment to be used in Johnson's own re-evaluation of the war. Wheeler came back this time with an outside request from Westmoreland for 206,000 more troops. Westmoreland claimed he needed the men to take maximum advantage of his position and press the battered enemy. There were recommendations for expanding the fighting into Cambodia and Laos.

Johnson's Riot Commission issued its report, a startling document which envisioned a fragmented nation of black and white societies unless something was done soon. The White House was uncharacteristically silent. Johnson, it turned out, was irritated that the report had failed to dwell on what his administration already had done to combat the ghetto problems. The report also, in the view of some administration spokesmen, failed to condemn in strong enough terms those who actually broke the laws.

The gold problem reached panic proportions, and the London market had to be closed and sales of gold restricted to banks. Dean Rusk's long-awaited testimony before the Senate Foreign Relations Committee failed to reveal any new thinking despite the pledge that policy was being re-evaluated. Johnson, in a candid talk to some students about domestic conditions, confessed, "We'll have a bad summer. We'll have several bad summers before we avert the deficiencies of centuries."

The President hunkered down in the White House, trying to ride out the storm. He was moody between the incidents which held him prisoner. Sometimes he was irritable and mean. Other times he exuded optimism and cheer to such an extent that it seemed phony and was. Often he looked and acted exhausted, both emotionally and physically. His eyes were red and rheumy from his hours of reading reports and intelligence cables. He had special lights installed in his bedroom, but there was little relief.

Security became an increasing problem. Johnson could not travel at ease in his land, the first President to be so contained. Sometimes he talked about the dozen men who had scaled the White House fence in the last year and been captured by the police on the grounds. There had been twelve thousand threatening letters in that year. He wanted to go into Washington's ghetto, but was barred by the Secret Service. He feared that to expose the Presidency to the harassment of pickets and protestors would erode respect for the office. His trips became confined to military bases and other secure areas. No advance notice of his travels was given. Even in his adopted city of Austin there was an ugly demonstration and a pop bottle was thrown at the Presidential motorcade.

Bobby Kennedy grew more feverish as dissent mounted and events cast a gloomy spell over the country. The week before the New Hampshire primary vote, Peter Lisagor and I had lunch with the Senator. He was not himself. The easy wit was gone. He sat at the table with eyes downcast and took only a halfhearted interest in the discussion. There was no tolerance of Lyndon Johnson. When the President was mentioned, Kennedy became emotional. He felt that Johnson's leadership had collapsed. He was despondent over the new recommendations for more troops. When the question about Kennedy renouncing candidacy came up, he suddenly looked up and shot us a blunt question: "Did I make a mistake?" Though both of us felt he had been wise to stay out, our answers hardly were important. For the first time Lisagor and I realized that Bob Kennedy was on the verge of changing his mind.

The next Tuesday New Hampshire went to the polls and the basic political weakness of Johnson was shown to the nation. Eugene McCarthy polled 42.2 percent of the vote (LBJ got 49.9 percent) and he lagged only 230 votes behind Johnson when Republican write-ins were added to the Democratic tally. The closed politics which Lyndon Johnson had brought to his party suddenly were ripped wide open. A sitting President could be challenged. Bob Kennedy called his strategists together both Tuesday and Wednesday nights in New York. He announced to the nation that he was actively reconsidering his position.

There was still strong inner counsel against his making the race. There was no thought that Johnson would step out. Though rumors about his health persisted, Johnson looked better than ever. He adhered to his diet with new tenacity and lost twenty or more pounds. Outwardly he seemed more determined than ever to cling to his course. He preached against divisiveness, asked America to stay the course as she had done in every war so far. Privately Walt Rostow's shop drew up memoranda pointing out that in the darkest hours victory often was only a short distance off. In the Civil War the South won some spectacular victories just before collapsing. So did Germany in World War I. The Battle of the Bulge was the last gasp of World War II. Bob Kennedy was aware of all of these things, but he had gotten a heady whiff of political revolution brewing in the grassroots.

Ted Sorensen, who had been John Kennedy's special counsel and speechwriter, worried over the delegate charts in his New York law office. He was opposed to Kennedy's entry, but he was ready to join his crusade if Kennedy decided to try it. Kenny O'Donnell, one of Bob Kennedy's oldest friends and an important political helper for John Kennedy, felt as Sorensen did. The

Senator's brother, Teddy Kennedy, had deep reservations. But Bob Kennedy's young staff and such disen-
chanted liberals as historian Schlesinger had long ago
urged him to run, and now they were more eager than
ever.

Kennedy could taste the battle. But there was one
more preliminary. Sorensen had arranged through his
friend W. De Vier Pierson, a White House aide, to see
Johnson. At this meeting Sorensen had bluntly expressed
his disenchantment with Johnson's policy and said that
there had to be a change to save the country from serious
fragmentation in a most critical time. Johnson replied
that he was open to ideas and he read off a list of the
prominent people he had consulted. Sorensen brought
up the idea of an independent commission of the most
able citizens for evaluating our position in Vietnam.
Johnson seemed interested and urged Sorensen to pursue
the idea. Together Sorensen and Kennedy devised a plan
which they took to Defense Secretary Clifford for trans-
mittal to Johnson. It was an offer from Kennedy to stay
out of the Democratic race if Johnson publicly promised
to alter his war policy. The debate no doubt will rage for
decades on whether such a proposal constituted an ulti-
matum to the President or whether it was a sincere ges-
ture by Robert Kennedy to subdue his immense ambition for what he considered the good of the nation. The
White House considered it akin to blackmail. Kennedy
considered it a reasonable and sensible political proposi-
tion.

What Sorensen and Kennedy brought to Clifford was

a proposal that the President name a commission com-
posed of the following men, or others like them: Yale
President Kingman Brewster, former Ambassador to
Japan Edwin O. Reischauer, former Deputy Secretary of
Defense Roswell Gilpatric, Generals Lauris Norstad and
Matthew Ridgway. All of these men had expressed strong
views opposed to Johnson's conduct of the war. Another
member of the commission was to be Robert Kennedy.
There is some confusion in later reports about whether
Kennedy insisted that he be a member, or be chairman,
or neither; at least he was proposed on the original
list. There was more discussion about membership.
The names of Senators Mike Mansfield, John Sherman
Cooper and George Aiken arose as men acceptable to
Kennedy and Sorensen. These three, too, had made no
secret of their opposition to Johnson's policy.

At the same time he named this group, the President
was to make public assurances that this was a genuine
commitment to redirect United States war policy. It was
not to be a publicity gimmick, another governmental
commission to be forgotten. Under such an arrangement,
Kennedy would not seek the Democratic nomination.

There is arrogance of such proportions in that propo-
sition as to awe the outside observer. And yet there is
also genuine sincerity, a conviction that a change of
policy was needed above everything else. It appears now
that Sorensen misread the signals from Lyndon Johnson.
The President manifests an interest in any new idea, if
for no other reason than to say that he has heard it.
There is no evidence that Johnson ever considered the

commission suggestion seriously.

Clifford dutifully took the proposal to Johnson. The rejection was swift and blunt. Johnson did not intend to assign Presidential authority to a commission. He did not intend to make such a political deal. He felt that such a move would destroy morale in Vietnam. He found the proposed panel to be stacked with doves. Less than forty-eight hours later Bob Kennedy had entered the race for the Democratic nomination and had begun to campaign.

The politicians at Johnson's side were appalled. The Kennedy threat was real. They did not believe that Kennedy could actually take the nomination away from a sitting President, but they worried that a fight for the nomination might tear up the party so severely that the Republican nominee could win. Johnson offered no hope for them. He remained as aloof as ever concerning politics. He talked now and then with Larry O'Brien and Jim Rowe, but he gave them no authority nor any plan. The White House's chief political operative remained Marvin Watson, a man devoid of any national political sensitivity.

Such political experts as Richard Scammon were at a loss to explain Johnson's indifference. Indeed, it was Scammon's contention that a minimum of interest and effort shown in New Hampshire might have changed the entire picture. New Hampshire was mechanically manageable, in Scammon's view. A well-organized campaign might have given 55 percent of the vote to Johnson and won him all the delegates. That would have deflated

McCarthy, perhaps kept Kennedy from entering the race.

Only that handful of people knew what was on Johnson's mind. Johnson wanted it to stay that way. Thus, as he prepared his new peace efforts and made his plans for his dramatic withdrawal from politics, Johnson also authorized his political machine to be geared up an extra notch or two. Watson moved out of the office next to Johnson, relinquishing his appointment duties to James Jones. Watson became a full-time political operative in another office. Men were dispatched to Wisconsin and California to bolster Johnson's efforts in those primaries. How sad the President's political condition was, was demonstrated in both states. The Johnson-Humphrey headquarters in California was largely deserted. Kennedy's new headquarters had lines of volunteers. In Wisconsin the Johnson groups had to hire office help because so few came on their own to work.

Nevertheless, even on the weekend when Johnson declared himself out, a team of men working on telephones in the Johnson-Humphrey Citizens offices in Washington reached the tentative conclusion that Johnson could have a maximum of 1700 delegates and a minimum of 1400. Only 1312 were needed for nomination. This information was relayed to Johnson only hours before he went on television.

The national reaction to his momentous announcement was varied. Most people liked the fact that he was out of politics and they gave him the benefit of any doubts they had about why he had done it. His popularity shot from 36 percent to 49 percent. Journalists were paralyzed. It was the third major political prognostication about which they had been wrong. (Romney's abortive candidacy and Rockefeller's early failure to declare were the other two.) Some pundits were swept with a wave of guilt feelings over the harsh things they had said about Johnson and they suddenly found new dimensions in the man. It was not a commendable season for punditry. Johnson partisans heaped the blame on the ambitions of Bob Kennedy. William S. White, the President's long-time friend and public apologist, called it a "bloodless assassination."

Fortunately, this bickering was short-lived. Events again intervened. On April 3 Johnson was chatting in his office with Washington's Senator Henry Jackson and his wife and children when an aide entered with the bulletin that Hanoi had agreed to meet and talk about a total bombing pause. This was the first fissure in the three-year wall of indifference which had so frustrated the President. There was no promise in the terse announcement of an end to fighting. Nor was the future really much clearer. But here at least was one step toward peace, a step which had been denied Johnson until he announced that he did not plan to run again for President. Without changing his expression, in a very calm voice he asked aide Tom Johnson to summon his top advisers to draft a response.

Only a little more than twenty-four hours later Martin Luther King was assassinated and violence swept across the nation. For the first time since the War of 1812 the smoke from a ravaged city could be smelled on the White House lawn. The eerie sound of sirens pierced the spring air of the capital and streets normally filled with government workers and shoppers were deserted under an early curfew. In the White House, after a slow start, Johnson worked quietly and quickly. Contingency plans for the mobilization of troops were instituted and Negro leaders were summoned for consultation. The pattern was repeated across the land. The flames and violence were muffled. The troops, though late in coming, moved with dispatch and restraint once on the scene. There was a minimum of killing. Order returned. And in the first pause at the end of that momentous week which saw politics and peace hopes and race relations all alter course, there was the sense that Lyndon Johnson had, by taking himself out of politics, served himself and his country well.

HUGH SIDEY

HUGH SIDEY is a fourth-generation journalist. His grandfather founded the *Adair County Free Press,* a weekly paper in Greenfield, Iowa, and the paper was subsequently owned and operated by his father and brother. Sidey learned the mechanical end of the business first—feeding presses, setting type and sweeping floors when he was still in grade school. Later he sold ads, wrote stories, took pictures and made the photoengravings. After a hitch in the Army at the end of World War II, he completed his education at Iowa State College, then began the classic journalistic migration from the heartland to Washington. Sidey broke in on the *Council Bluffs* (Iowa) *Nonpareil,* for which he covered every type of story, then moved across the Missouri River to *The Omaha World-Herald* and for four years reported from City Hall. His next move was to New York and a two-year stint with *Life,* and then to Washington, D.C., where he was White House correspondent and deputy bureau chief for *Time.* His previous book, *John F. Kennedy, President,* was published in 1963, and an amended edition appeared after the President's death. He now writes a weekly column, "The Presidency," for *Life* and lives in Maryland with his wife and three daughters.